The Illustrated History of
EDINBURGH'S SUBURBS

The Illustrated History of
EDINBURGH'S SUBURBS

SANDY MULLAY

breedon **books**
PUBLISHING

First published in Great Britain in 2002 by
The Breedon Books Publishing Company Limited
Breedon House, 3 The Parker Centre,
Derby, DE21 4SZ.

ISBN 1 85983 300 4

Printed and bound by Butler & Tanner, Frome, Somerset,
England.
Cover printing by Lawrence-Allen Colour Printers, Weston-
super-Mare, Somerset.

CONTENTS

Acknowledgments

I would like to thank the following for their help in the preparation of this book – Malcolm Cant, Stuart Sellar, Hamish Stevenson, Alwyn Coupe, Ian Taylor, Marilyn Mullay. Many thanks too to the staff of the Edinburgh Room, especially Ann Nix and Andrew Bethune, at the Central Library, as well as Peter Milne and his colleagues at the National Library of Scotland Map Division. Also, Rupert Harding and Susan Last for being such understanding editors. The maps in this volume are reproduced courtesy of the Trustees of the National Library of Scotland.

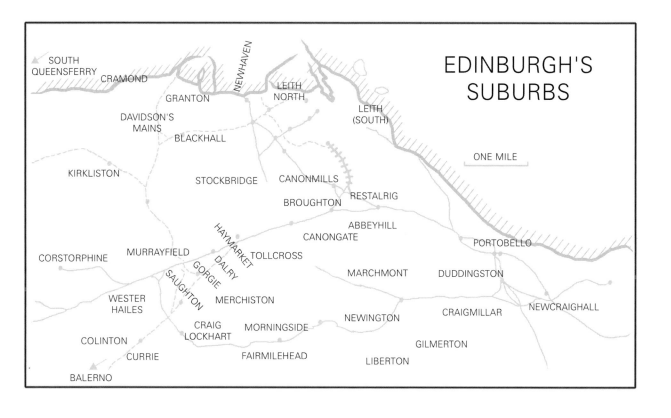

Introduction

Edinburgh is the UK's favourite city. That was the conclusion of two opinion polls recently conducted among international travellers by English-based newspapers. This is a major achievement for a city without a truly international airport and deprived of a motorway link with the south. It does not even boast a major television studio to help it send out the message that Edinburgh is well worth a visit. Yet it persists in the traveller's imagination as a city which must be seen and sampled.

But to the resident, Edinburgh is something else. Edinburgh is an accumulation of districts, some of them former villages and even independent burghs, others planned developments on the periphery of the conurbation. They represent the Edinburgh that the visitor may never see, but they represent the reality of Edinburgh nevertheless. And it is a diverse reality.

Former independent burghs like Leith and Portobello rub shoulders with 20th-century developments like Craigmillar and Wester Hailes, which have had to forge their own identities and culture. One-time villages like Colinton and Duddingston have fought to maintain their unique identities – and have succeeded or failed in equal measure. Well-known communities on the fringe of Edinburgh – such as Ratho and South Queensferry – have, rightly or wrongly, shown a wariness about being drawn into the conurbation just outside their former boundaries. Indeed, the independently-minded Musselburgh, just a few miles east of Princes Street, has successfully resisted being absorbed.

So this book will tell you about the real Edinburgh as only its residents can see it. Forget the tartan dolls, the Edinburgh rock, the too-colourful postcards; this is the Edinburgh of tenements, housing schemes, schools and libraries. Hopefully, it is also the Edinburgh of the history books – for much of Scotland's history has taken place in Edinburgh outside the city centre.

It was on the Burgh Moor, in present-day Marchmont, that the Scottish army assembled to begin its fateful march to Flodden. It was in Leith that George IV, the first Hanoverian monarch to visit Scotland, tentatively landed, following in the footsteps of Mary Stewart (Mary Queen of Scots as she is usually known), neither of them quite knowing how the natives would react. It was at Swanston that Stevenson wrote one of his most famous novels, and in Duddingston that the famous *Encyclopedia Britannica* was moulded into an intellectual bestseller. It was at Newhaven and Joppa that Darwin began to grasp the multiplicity of life in a rock pool, and at Blackford that telescopes scanned the night sky for 80 years.

Mention of Charles Darwin underlines how Edinburgh's suburbs have been frequented by some of the most important luminaries of Scottish – and British – history. As Darwin was to biology, so James Hutton was to geology; indeed he has been described as the 'founder' of the modern science. This Edinburgh-born

Welcome to Edinburgh. Motorists driving into the capital on the former A1 road from Musselburgh are greeted by this splendid 1960s sign, complete with the arms of the former town council.

scientist hailed from the St Leonard's district, then part of Canongate. Earlier than this, Merchiston could make a claim for considerable recognition in the world of scientific achievement through its famed resident John Napier. Not content with pioneering logarithms, Napier went on to produce a mechanical computing device – an excellent excuse for modern Edinburgh to open a museum of computing, surely, although none is planned at the time of writing.

James Clerk-Maxwell, one of the most important physicists who has ever lived, attended school in the Canonmills area of the city. Incidentally, he took the world's first colour photograph and this is highly appropriate for someone born and raised in Scotland's capital, since pioneer Calotype photographers Hill and Adamson did most of their work in Edinburgh. Newhaven and Colinton were locations for their 'sun pictures' as they were called, but Hill's photographic work had begun with a commission to paint the ministers setting up the Free Kirk in the Canonmills area in 1843.

Authors such as Robert Louis Stevenson and Sir Arthur Conan Doyle were both born in the city and are both associated with individual districts – Conan Doyle with Broughton, where his creation Sherlock Holmes surveys a huge traffic island, and Stevenson with Swanston, where the author of *Treasure Island* spent many happy summers in the Pentland-side village. Stevenson will also feature in the Canonmills story, since he enjoyed the funfair there. And to bring the literary history of Edinburgh almost up to date, we have to note Irvine Welsh writing about Leith, and none other than J.K. Rowling in the Comely Bank area (Stockbridge). Merchiston has recently lost its literary queen, the much-lamented Dorothy Dunnett, who wrote her mediaeval sagas just along the road from Napier's tower-house.

How is this book arranged? *Edinburgh's Suburbs* is configured in A-Z order around 37 districts listed. Most of these have been identified by the local authority as viable enough to elect their own community council. Many of them have failed to take advantage of the legislation allowing them to do so, but this designation is nevertheless a useful measure of their stature as mutually exclusive areas. Leith and Portobello are too important to divide up and are given pride of place as exclusive entities. As the book's title implies, this text is about suburbs – that is, districts 'under' the city of Edinburgh in the sense of being satellites to the centre of Edinburgh.

So, if you wish to read about Edinburgh Castle, Greyfriar's Bobby and the Scott Monument, you must do so elsewhere (and a bibliography is included to help you find such information). But if you want to read about Leith's record of shipping and shipbuilding, about the 1930s Portobello swimming pool big enough to house two modern Olympic facilities, about Hearts and Hibs, ice-hockey at Murrayfield and athletics at Meadowbank, about the building of the world's greatest bridge and about kingfishers and otters on the city's rivers, then this book is for you.

Chronological guide to the municipal expansion of Edinburgh

1296	Edinburgh recorded in English invasion documents.
1329	Leith harbour awarded to Edinburgh by Robert the Bruce.
1603	Charter status awarded by James VI.
	Royal court leaves Edinburgh for London.
1707	Scottish Parliament leaves Edinburgh for London.
1833	Leith and Portobello awarded burgh status – split from Edinburgh.
1856	Absorbed Canongate, Calton, Portsburgh.
1896	Absorbed Portobello.
1920	Amalgamated with Leith. Absorbed Colinton and Corstorphine.
1974	Absorbed Currie, Balerno, Ratho, South Queensferry.
1975	City of Edinburgh District Council formed, sharing local government duties with Lothian Region.
1996	Lothian Region abolished. City of Edinburgh Council formed.
1999	Scottish Parliament up and running.

A brief history of the development of Edinburgh

When was Edinburgh first established? The interested enquirer can begin by discounting the notion that the city had been in existence for 330 years before the birth of Christ. This was the modest claim made by the magistrates in 1618 in a loyal address to King James VI. In the previous century, an English historian proclaimed that the city had been founded no less than 889 years BC. Modern historians treat these claims with caution, indeed, disbelief!

Nevertheless, prehistoric occupation of the Castle Rock may go back as far as 7,000 years, this prominent residue of volcanic activity offering safety and military supremacy to whoever occupied it. It is believed that the Votadini tribe counted the rock among their Lothian fortress sites, but it seems to have held no appeal for the Roman legions, who preferred to concentrate their activities in the Edinburgh area on occupying the Esk and Almond river mouths. As a result, it is Cramond, and not the city centre, that can surprise the archaeologist with finds of Roman remains, as happened spectacularly just a few years ago, with the discovery of a handsome leonine statue.

Edinburgh's earliest years as a municipality are not fully documented, historians usually regarding Edward I's demand in 1296 for the city's allegiance, signed by alderman Edward de Dederyk, as evidence that the community was substantial enough to merit such attention.

Over the decades, the city's early history was tied closely to that of the royal court, even before capital status was officially recognised, if only because of the importance of the castle. The town's early development was 'geology-led', a densely-inhabited complex of buildings adhering to the volcanic 'crag and tail' formation stretching eastwards from the rising fortification. (A similar landform can be seen at Blackford, with the Royal Observatory in the 'Holyrood' position.) With ordinary people's dwellings springing up outside the castle gates, it was not surprising that a street began to form down the ridge eastwards to what is now Holyrood.

From its establishment by David I in 1128, Holyrood rose to prominence, first as an abbey, then later as a royal palace, giving the Royal Mile the accolade of the most important High Street in the kingdom: castle at one end, abbey then palace at the other, while one-quarter of the way down was the first custom-built parliament building. Although only used for some 70 years, this still stands, and is soon to be shadowed by the new Scottish Parliament building presently taking shape at the Holyrood end of the High Street – ironically in what used to be Canongate, a municipality separate from Edinburgh (and treated in this book as an Edinburgh suburb).

In 1603, the year when James VI took his court to London, he granted a charter to Edinburgh confirming its rights and privileges. Known as the Golden

Charter, this outlined the boundaries of the royal burgh, by no means an academic exercise when this municipal status effectively prevented any nearby community from challenging any of the monopolies enshrined in the charter. The boundaries were stipulated as running from Edgebuckling Brae (the east end of Musselburgh links) on the east, to the River Almond on the west, and from the southern limit of the Sheriffdom of Edinburgh northwards to the middle of the Forth.

This of course included the port of Leith – the most important in Scotland after the English took permanent possession of Berwick in the 15th century – and it experienced a difficult relationship with its parent city throughout its history. Originally gifted to Edinburgh by Robert the Bruce in 1329, the year of his death, the administration of harbour dues ensured a near-strangling of the port which infuriated Leithers and still baffles historians. This summed up Edinburgh's relationship with Leith – promoting it as a major port, while wary, even envious, of its success. The construction of a fort there during the 17th century did nothing to make Leith's relationship with Edinburgh any less intense, and this matter will be examined in more detail in the chapter on Leith. Suffice to say that, when investment in Leith's docks threatened Edinburgh's financial equilibrium in the 1820s and 30s, the Scottish capital was quick to release Leith from its sphere of influence. The port became an independent burgh from 1833 to 1920, before being re-absorbed. But more of that later.

Other burghs taken into Edinburgh over the years were closer to the city's heart. A walled city for much of its history, Edinburgh occupied the Castle Rock ridge only as far down as the Nethergate, just below John Knox's house nowadays, with the independent burgh of Canongate occupying the lower part of the ridge down to Holyrood. Separate little municipalities sprung up immediately around the 'city centre' in the form of the baronies of Portsburgh and Calton. Little remains of these nowadays, but more substantial annexations to Edinburgh include such well-known placenames as Portobello on the east, and Dalmeny, South Queensferry, Kirkliston and Ratho on the west. Of these, Queensferry was no less than a royal burgh, with Portobello enjoying burgh status in the 19th century.

In contrast, 20th-century additions to Edinburgh have largely taken the form of planned 'schemes' of council housing. While offering more amenable accommodation than previously available in the slums of Leith or the city's Canongate and Cowgate, the districts of Craigmillar, Pilton, Muirhouse and Wester Hailes lacked the obvious shopping and recreational facilities which their new inhabitants could reasonably have expected.

As a result of this geographical expansion, the population of Edinburgh has increased steadily throughout the last 150 years, but without the dramatic upsurge that characterised, for example, the growth of Glasgow. Indeed, Edinburgh was overtaken by the latter city by the beginning of the 19th century, when shipbuilding and manufacturing, both highly labour-intensive occupations, created even greater manpower demands than Edinburgh's, namely banking, life assurance and the professions of medicine, education, and law.

Without a dramatic increase brought on through industrialisation, it is difficult not to relate the increase in Edinburgh's population figures to the spread of the city into its hinterland, although the general increase in longevity caused by more stable food provision and water supply services must also be taken into account in assessing population growth.

Because of the differing fates of Edinburgh's parishes, it is not possible to simply add parochial population figures to the city's whenever an outlying community was added to the capital. Cramond, for example, has declined as an industrial site and has been surpassed in this respect by Granton, once a satellite of Cramond. Similarly, Duddingston was the parochial capital for an area of eastern Edinburgh stretching from Restalrig almost to Musselburgh at one time, so it is clear that the traditional population pattern broke down as the Industrial Revolution proceeded, and, equally, the agricultural community receded. Between the censuses of 1851 and 1981 Edinburgh's population approximately doubled, from around 190,000 to 390,000, in which time the city absorbed its surrounding baronies of Canongate, Calton, and Portsburgh (all in 1856), Portobello (40 years later), Leith, Corstorphine and Colinton in 1920, and Currie, Balerno, Ratho and South Queensferry some 55 years after that.

Not surprisingly, Edinburgh can claim to be Scotland's largest city, in area, if not population. With an area of 26,080 hectares it outstrips Dundee with 23,504 and is well ahead of its rival Glasgow, which covers a mere 19,790 hectares. The latter city has no fewer than twice as many inhabitants to the hectare as the capital – 33.5 in Glasgow, 16.1 in Edinburgh, so the latter can claim to offer its inhabitants more elbow room than any other Scottish city. Another characteristic of the population figures is the outnumbering of males by females, in a ratio of around 19:22, probably accounted for by the high proportion of citizens living in Edinburgh beyond retirement age, in which age group there is always a numerical superiority in favour of women.

Like most cities, Edinburgh's population is actually in decline, although this fall has not gone much over the 1% mark annually, in contrast to Glasgow's whopping 15% loss in the 1980s. While it might appear that Edinburgh's decline will be stopped, or even reversed, by the establishment of the Scottish Parliament, with all the support services that it will inevitably create, this political innovation has led to a deliberate policy of decentralisation. Edinburgh's water, for example, will no longer be administered by the city which pioneered urban water supply in 17th-century Scotland – the new headquarters for Edinburgh's, and all Scotland's, water will be based in Dunfermline.

While this decentralisation policy is all very well in theory, it should be remembered that Edinburgh has never been allowed to dominate Scottish life in the manner London does England's. Indeed, watching BBC or STV news bulletins being beamed from Glasgow, you would hardly know that Edinburgh existed at all. Edinburgh has so much less to lose than its English capital counterpart, and the policy of establishing Government offices away from the city should be viewed with caution. As this book will make clear, the city's suburbs have lost many important industries, such as crystal-making (Abbeyhill), confectionery (Broughton), printing and publishing (Abbeyhill, Newington), newspaper (Canonmills), and rubber (Dalry). The beneficiaries are the communities of Penicuik, West Lothian, Motherwell and Glasgow. How many of their industries have been relocated to Edinburgh, one is forced to ask?

The present city council has 58 members, nearly double the figure for 1800. This stood at 33 and remained constant for 50 years, even through 1833, a year which was something of a watershed for elected government in the United Kingdom. The passing of the Reform Act at Westminster in 1832 led to a similar measure for Scotland the following year. While this provided only a partial extension of the size of the voting population – and certainly failed to satisfy popular agitation on the matter – it was sufficient to introduce a series of such measures which led to the complete democracy we know today. Local government was included in this gradual process of democratisation, and, in a purely local context, led to the establishment of Leith and Portobello as independent burghs.

That Leith's independence was hastily granted is not difficult to discern, nor is the fact that the Edinburgh ratepayers found it highly convenient! No town hall was immediately available, the new Sherrif Court being hurriedly converted, while the matter of raising local revenue had been completely overlooked. Even with the port being represented in Parliament by the Lord Advocate, some five years were to pass before the new burgh was able to raise its own revenue.

It was at this time that Edinburgh entered into the murkiest period of its municipal history; a time of financial incompetence which led to the city being declared bankrupt. Following years of irregular bookkeeping it was discovered in 1799 that the City Chamberlain of 30 years standing had no grasp of the capital's financial affairs. This crisis brought Edinburgh to the brink of insolvency, and the building of Leith Docks pushed it over. A Government loan for their construction carried ruinous penalties, leading to the Exchequer obtaining virtually all the benefits accruing from the new facility. Leith's 'independence' in 1833 was an attempt to regularise the fiscal position, the history of which has proved difficult to trace over the years because of the chaotic state of the city's financial records.

The Town Council moved into the City Chambers, then the Royal Exchange, in 1811, but did not have exclusive use of the building until 1893. Previously, it had been used as a government Customs House, as well as containing coffee houses, shops and the Royal Bank of Scotland. It was built in 1754–61 over three closes, Stewart's, Pearson's and Mary King's, the last of which still exists underneath the chambers as an early example of a street museum.

By the 1820s Lord Cockburn was describing the Town Council as 'omnipotent, corrupt, impenetrable' adding for good measure 'silent, powerful, submissive, mysterious, and irresponsible'. (The submissiveness was probably to the 'uncrowned' government minister Henry Dundas.) Cockburn was a Whig (Liberal); the 33 town councillors Tories to a man (32 elected, plus the Dean of Guild), a not insignificant fact at the time of the general election in 1833, when they were the only parliamentary voters in the city.

In 1856, Edinburgh began to recover lost ground with the absorption by the city of the separate burgh of Canongate and the baronies of Calton and Portsburgh, effectively all the cityward area administered by the police commissioners, effectively extending local democracy. Forty years later, the independent burgh of Portobello was absorbed – not entirely with its inhabitants' approval – but this measure of civic displeasure was as nothing compared to the public reaction to the 'amalgamation' of Leith with Edinburgh in 1920. Effectively an annexation, this civic merging is dealt with in more detail in the section on Leith, and is well documented in the works of historian James Marshall. Leith's town clerk conducted a referendum, then known as a plebiscite, which showed a majority against the amalgamation, but the legality of the survey was questioned.

In this year, 1920, Colinton and Corstorphine were absorbed into Edinburgh, which was already supplying basic municipal services anyway. Ten years later, Edinburgh, newly designated as one of the four city authorities in Scotland, took on responsibilities for education, mental health and poor law, previously administered by autonomous boards. This status remained unchanged until 1975 with the introduction of the two-tier system of local government. The City of Edinburgh District Council was responsible for such matters as planning, recreation and refuse collection, while losing high-spending responsibilities such as education, social work and transport to Lothian Region for the period 1975–96. The public responded surprisingly positively to what could have been a highly confusing dichotomy of service provision, but even the public's patience failed to prevent another reorganisation coming along only 20 years later. This saw the re-creation of unitary bodies such as the City of Edinburgh Council, but even more responsibilities, like water provision, were handed over to statutory bodies. Losing one tier of local government was probably a useful preparatory step before the establishment of the Scottish Parliament, although the party in power at Westminster at that time had no such intention!

Meanwhile, the 1970s reorganisation had brought in three communities to the west which were formerly administratively in West Lothian or Midlothian, but were now deemed to have increasingly come under the shadow of the Scottish capital. Ratho and Kirkliston are separated from Edinburgh now only by green belt, but South Queensferry, a former royal burgh of some antiquity, still has an air of independence about it. (Nevertheless, you will find it listed in *Edinburgh's Suburbs*!) For a list of local government wards and the chapters which cover them in this book, see Appendix.

The enlargement of Edinburgh has had little or no effect on the city's politics;

the political landscape here is as red as almost everywhere else in Scotland. Until 1833 Edinburgh had one MP, invariably Tory, elected by no more than 32 voters – town councillors – most of whom were Tory too. The First Reform Act, however, made matters a little more interesting, with two members being returned, and with numerous by-elections taking place whenever a sitting member was given a Government post, as required by the electoral laws of the day.

Liberals held both Edinburgh seats at every election for the next 50 years, while Leith was a Liberal burgh throughout its history as an independent municipality (1833–1920). Two more seats were allocated to Edinburgh in 1885, and the four were arranged geographically – central, south, east and west. All were staunchly Liberal; no Tory captured a seat until 1909, in the West constituency, and no Labour candidate did so until the 'Khaki Election' of 1918, when Central returned a Socialist. In the same year a North seat was created, with Pentlands being established in 1950.

Edinburgh was overcome by successive waves of Conservatism and (supposedly) Socialism. No Liberal held a seat in Edinburgh from 1945 until 1997, while the Tories did reasonably well, holding a majority of seats in 1959, with the exception of Central, East, and Leith. But by 1997 the blue flame was extinguished in the city, although the Liberals won back Edinburgh West in that year.

Did the suburbanisation of Edinburgh's hinterland throw up any political phenomena? The answer is in the affirmative. In 1927 Captain Wedgwood Benn decided to convert his '–isms' from Liberal to Social in 'crossing the floor', forcing a by-election in his own seat of Leith, something which is never done nowadays by politicians changing parties. The good voters of Leith decided they wanted none of this Socialist nonsense, and threw out this hard-working MP, nowadays better remembered as the father of Tony Benn. Leith finally changed to Labour in 1945 and has never been anything else since.

Pentlands, a constituency encompassing the Water of Leith communities from Juniper Green to Balerno as well as a swathe of south-west Edinburgh from Wester Hailes to Fairmilehead, established itself as a footnote in psephological histories when it unseated Malcolm (now Sir Malcolm) Rifkind, the Foreign Secretary, in 1997. He became the most senior politician to lose his seat in Britain since 1906, and it is hard to image a more centralised Edinburgh constituency acting so dramatically as did the voters resident in these former Midlothian villages. Admittedly, Edinburgh South saw a Labour MP oust a Conservative minister in 1987, but since the sitting member – Michael Ancrum – had been responsible for introducing the Community Charge (or Poll Tax as even Mrs Thatcher referred to it), it is perhaps hardly surprising!

The outward growth of Edinburgh can be chronicled with some accuracy by the extension of the old tram system into the suburbs – and for this reason the author makes no apologies for including some of Stuart Sellar's fine tram illustrations in this volume. Alan Brotchie's recent updating of the late David Hunter's classic work *Edinburgh's Transport* illustrates the expansion of the city's transport network, and of course by implication, the city itself.

Consider that Edinburgh's transport system came under full municipal control in 1919, amalgamated with Leith's the following year (the capital's cable rolling-stock being outshone by the port's electric vehicles), and then, following full electrification, spread out into the suburbs. Corstorphine and Colinton were absorbed by Edinburgh in 1920, and became part of the electric tram network by 1923 and 1926 respectively. On the other hand, Slateford was still surrounded by green fields when the trams reached there in 1927, but not all outlying areas benefited, with Gilmerton and Balerno having to make to do with the motor bus. Musselburgh bucked the trend by refusing to consider joining with Edinburgh despite the sight of the city's tram cars reaching Levenhall, at the far end of Musselburgh racecourse.

The increase of Edinburgh Corporation bus and tram routes, from 51 miles in 1929 to 70 in 1939 and to 123 in 1961 tells its own story (and of course, the 1961 mileage figure was for buses only, trams last running in Edinburgh and its environs in 1956). The 1986 deregulation of the British bus industry brought such 'distant' areas as Dalkeith and Tranent into the ambit of Edinburgh's buses, although the scheme caused chaos on many routes taken over by 'out of town' operators, whose drivers often had to be guided by their passengers!

The story of the rail network is, in contrast, one of total decline as far as commuter journeys are concerned. In all, Edinburgh has lost more than 50 passenger stations within the city boundary; nowadays it has only four remaining (excluding such central stations as Waverley and Haymarket). In 1925 a local newspaper predicted that Edinburgh would lose its suburban network if the Waverley Station – deep in its glen between Old and New Towns – did not soon have escalators to spare the exertions of regular commuters. The newspaper was absolutely correct!

The Granton branch closed in that year, South Queensferry and Kirkliston four years later, with Balerno, North Leith, Barnton, and Leith Central all losing their passenger services within a 10-year period from 1942. The 1960s saw the withdrawal of services to and from Musselburgh (taking in Portobello and Joppa), the Suburban Circle (eight stations at once!), with Corstorphine following at the end of that decade. Even the new Edinburgh Crossrail service to and from Newcraighall is designed to cater for park-and-ride commuters from outside the city; the suburbs will not benefit directly. Indeed, there is reason to assume that Crossrail was prioritised over any possible reopening of the Suburban Circle, which would have directly benefited Edinburgh's council tax payers by offering them an immediate transport option.

Nowadays Edinburgh is a capital city without a mile of underground railway, a mere handful of suburban stations, and no modern tramway. With Scotland's railways administered from Glasgow since the late 1960s, it is perhaps no surprise that the decline in rail facilities has gone uncorrected, when escalators to Princes Street, or a 'moving pavement' up to Waverley Bridge could work wonders as a first step to restoring rail traffic to and from Edinburgh's suburbs. A more locally-driven concerted approach to solving the city's transport problems would surely include the establishment of a public transport executive, which Glasgow and its hinterland enjoy uniquely at the present time.

One measure of a community's stature lies in the way it treats its wildlife, and in this Edinburgh has a distinctly mixed record. While much of the local environment has improved with the 'greening' effect following the closure of so many mills and factories, the city council has perhaps done less than it should to further conservation measures in the city's green places. The city's parks appear threadbare and litter-strewn (to be fair, most of Britain's urban parks are like this), and the Countryside Rangers' Service, based at Hermitage House, is seriously starved of financial backing. Although the outgoing district council identified some 30 sites of natural history interest in Edinburgh, only two have been declared as local nature reserves at the time of writing – at Corstorphine Hill and Hermitage of Braid – and the city council shamefully uses these very sites for firework displays at Hogmanay. Despite all this, the otter and kingfisher are back on Edinburgh's rivers, fox and badger go about their business unheeded, and buzzard and osprey can be seen overhead. Edinburgh just needs to try a little harder!

Bibliographical Note

Mention will be noted of the *Statistical Accounts* and these of course are not peculiar to Edinburgh, but cover the whole of Scotland. They comprise a survey of the parishes of Scotland at three particular periods in history – the 1790s, 1840s, and immediately post-World War Two. The idea was that each minister would write an account of his parish – its location, wildlife, agriculture, industry, health and population factors, and sources of entertainment – this last category often an excuse for a good old-fashioned rant!

Edinburgh is arranged by parish in the first two surveys (the index in the first *Account* is bound in volume 20, not in 21, the final volume, although a modern facsimile edition from EP Publishing sensibly brings these together by city, a system adopted for the *New*, or *Second*, *Account*). The *Third Account* is a single-volume work published in 1966, and edited on a non-parish basis. When this author wrote his *Edinburgh Encyclopedia*, he found the '3SA' invaluable, even although much of the data was by then out of date.

ABBEYHILL

Origin of name: believed topographical.
Government: (local) covered by Holyrood and Meadowbank
wards (34 & 35) of Edinburgh City Council;
(national) Edinburgh Central and North & Leith
constituencies. No community council.

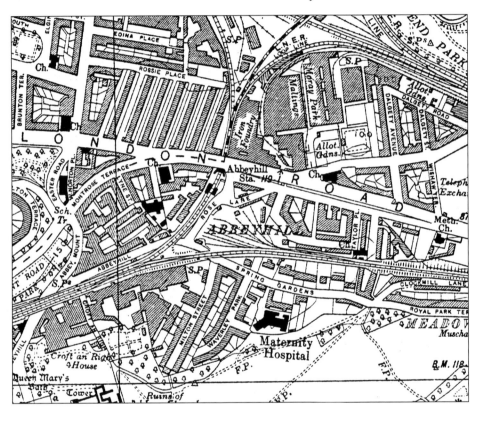

Opposite page:
Abbeymount overlooks
Holyrood Palace, but
this is the view in the
opposite direction –
northwards towards
Easter Road. The bus
enthusiast will be
delighted with this
1958 shot, showing as
it does two different
generations of vehicle
on the 1/21 services.
Single-deckers had to be
used on these routes
because of the low
railway bridges between
here and Holyrood, and
also at the foot of
Easter Road.
(Edinburgh City
Libraries)

No such parish as Abbeyhill is recorded in the *First* or *Second Statistical Accounts*, although the *First* volume records 'Abbay Hill' as the eastern boundary of Edinburgh in 1792. Abbeyhill probably began as a dormitory for staff servicing Holyrood, firstly in its ecclesiastical role, then in its royal one. The present suburb is very much a product of the 19th century Industrial Revolution, as a glance at the high-density housing stock will show.

Occupying the ridge immediately to the north of Holyrood Abbey, and part of the slope stretching away to the Forth from there, Abbeyhill stands on a fork where incoming road traffic from Portobello or the A1 divides to make for Leith Walk, or to the east end of Princes Street. Leith lies to the north, and the town council minutes of 1500 record that, when plague raged in Leith, Edinburgh carters would dump their cargoes at Abbeymount on the 'easter road' to the port, and Leith carriers would collect the cargoes there. Eastwards, a new retail park nowadays leads into Marionville and Meadowbank.

Any photographer attempting to take this Abbeyhill view in daylight hours nowadays would be lucky to survive! This is the middle of the A1, seen coming down from Abbeymount to the left, although London Road, to the right, carries a greater volume of traffic. This 1957 photograph shows that the tram lines are still in situ, although the overhead catenary has gone, the last trams having run to Joppa in the summer of the previous year. A policeman on points duty sufficed to handle what traffic there was – and that year began with a petrol shortage – but nowadays traffic lights are essential at this important junction. (Anne Campbell, on behalf of J. Campbell Harper)

Meadowbank – wedged between Abbeyhill, Piershill, and Restalrig, is the site of Scotland's most important sports centre. Meadowbank stadium opened in May 1970, inheriting the sites of Old and New Meadowbank. The former was a banked stadium with a cinder track used for speedway (which moved to Powderhall, but has now emigrated to West Lothian) and Leith Athletic FC (now defunct), while the latter catered mainly for athletics. And it was athletics which featured at the brand-new stadium, with its 23,000 all-seater capacity. Here the Commonwealth Games of 1970 and 1986 were held; the former was a triumph, with Scotland accumulating a respectable mass of medals in an atmosphere of friendly competition. Sixteen years later, the clouds descended – literally and metaphorically. Racked by bad weather and financial maladministration, the 1986 event has opened an as yet unclosed chapter of non-achievement for Scottish athletes, the honourable exception being Liz McColgan, who, as Liz Lynch, brought a touch of sunlight to the 1986 Edinburgh games by winning the 10,000 metres.

From the 19th century, Abbeyhill was a highly industrious area, replete with tenements and 'colony' style housing, but now a number of local industries (printing, glassmaking) have either moved out to Midlothian, or closed down altogether (metalworking at London Road Foundry). The 'colonies' here are still a feature of local housing, and much sought-after, and there is an appropriately named 'Artisan's Bar' at the end of one row, located right on the A1. (Although for fine pub architecture, look for the Stag and Turret Inn on Abbeymount.)

Abbeyhill's railway station, which could hardly have been more centrally

situated, closed in 1963, depriving citizens of the chance of reaching Waverley in barely four minutes. This was the northern leg of the 'Sub' railway, so destinations on the south side, from Craigmillar across to Gorgie, are also no longer easily attainable. Present-day buses link with the city centre either along London Road and Leith Street, or, less frequently, by Regent Road. Both routes take more than four minutes to reach Princes Street.

A name once synonymous with Abbeyhill was Else Inglis. Dr Inglis was a brave and resourceful doctor who was determined to place her skills at the service of her country in World War One, but was prevented from entering the Western Front war theatre by the War Office. Undaunted, she took her hospital unit – staffed almost entirely by women – to Serbia and Russia, providing the best medical services she could in harrowing conditions. Struck down by cancer in 1917, she was buried in Edinburgh, crowds standing eight deep on Princes Street to see her cortège pass, such was her fame. The maternity hospital which carried her name opened in 1925, but failed to survive the medical rationalising processes which broke out in the 1980s and closed in 1988. Unfortunately, the papers and records of her unique wartime enterprise were left to a library in the west of Scotland, which, at the time of writing, seems unable to catalogue them.

Surprisingly, Abbeyhill holds an important place in the UK's aeronautical history, for it was from here at the Comely Garden, a pleasure park where Lower

This 1950 photograph of Abbeyhill perfectly illustrates two contrasting types of housing. 'Colony'-style houses are to the fore on both left and right, in Maryfield Place and Alva Place, with fairly standard tenements in Rossie Place, at right angles at the end of the street. The horse-drawn milk float was a familiar sight in some parts of Edinburgh for another two decades. (Edinburgh City Libraries)

Just down London Road from Abbeyhill is Meadowbank, the national athletics stadium opened in time for the 1970 Commonwealth Games, and host for a second time in 1986. From the road it is obvious, from the missing lettering of the stadium's name, and the panel hanging off, that its best days are past. Its facilities fail to meet the demands of modern sports arenas, and at the time of writing the playing-field at its centre is used by Hibernian reserves.

London Road is now, that the first balloon flight began on the British mainland. On 27 August 1784 Edinburgh polymath James Tytler lifted off in a basket under the 'Great Edinburgh Fire Balloon'. The daring aeronaut had exhibited his balloon within the incomplete hall of Register House in order to raise funding, but technical difficulties meant that the first take-off had been postponed a number of times. Presumably, this was because the envelope, 40ft high by 30ft wide, and made of animal skins, was not as airtight as he had hoped. Nevertheless, Tytler persevered.

Flying for about 10 minutes, Tytler reached a height of 350 feet and landed safely at nearby Restalrig. Despite his achievement – eclipsed locally by the visiting Lunardi in the following year – Tytler is better remembered, if at all, for his work on the *Encyclopedia Britannica*, undertaken at Duddingston. It is as well that he has this publication as some kind of monument; there is none dedicated to him in Edinburgh, and a recently-published reference book on aviation firmly credits James Sadler of Oxford as Britain's first balloonist. In fact, Tytler preceded him by six weeks, but that too is forgotten.

BALERNO

Origin of name: Believed from the Gaelic, meaning 'farm with sloe bushes'.
Government: (local) ward 1, Balerno, also community council; (national) Edinburgh Pentlands constituency.

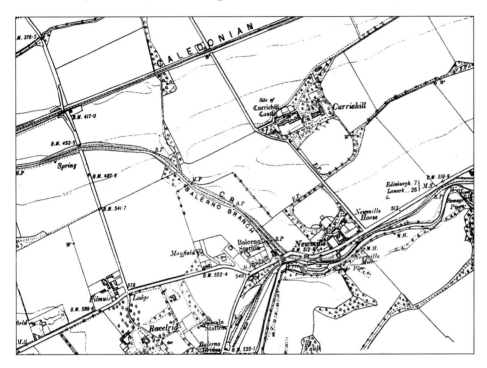

Nowadays very much a dormitory of Edinburgh, Balerno, some seven miles south-west of the city, has a long history as an independent community at the highest point on the Water of Leith, where its water could be put to work. Corn mills are recorded here from the 14th century and paper mills from the 18th. Additionally, a freestone quarry fed Edinburgh's building frenzy in the final quarter of the 18th century.

At that time, the village of Balerno was part of Currie parish, and shared with the latter a splendid longevity of its citizenship. Writing in 1845, the Currie minister recorded that Balerno's William Napier, who lived to a modest 112, 'was an excellent pedestrian' who could out-distance a horse, and years after celebrating his centenary, could still scythe grass daily for his cow.

Balerno was part of Midlothian until 1975, when it was absorbed by Edinburgh. The original village now has its main street pedestrianised; interestingly, this thoroughfare runs north-to-south, in contrast to the other two Water of Leith villages, Juniper Green and Currie, whose east-west main streets have been incorporated into the trunk road. Balerno has now been supplemented by bungalow housing to the south, with the population virtually quadrupling

In contrast to its near
neighbours Currie and
Juniper Green, the
main street at Balerno
runs north-south
instead of east-west.
Also unlike the others it
is pedestrianised,
although shoppers seem
few and far between
when this picture was
taken on a Thursday
morning. However, the
Co-op at the foot of the
brae was doing good
business, so the camera
is not telling the whole
story in this case.

Looking north from the
foot of the
pedestrianised main
street, the northern
approach to Balerno is
pictured. The town was
popular with American
servicemen during the
Cold War, when the
nearby Kirknewton
base was used by the
USAF.

since the 1961 census. The village was connected to Princes Street by rail from
1874 until the late 1960s, passenger trains last running in 1943. So awkwardly
curved was the line, taking in Colinton, Juniper Green and Currie on its sinuous
course, that as late as 1922 new four-wheel coaching stock was designed for use
on it, bogie carriages being unable to cope with the line's radii. First-class
passengers could rest their feet on velvet pile rugs, something that modern bus
passengers have to do without!

Balerno enjoys easy access to the Pentlands. Between 700 and 1,000ft up in these hills, not far south of the village, are two of Edinburgh's best-known reservoirs, Threipmuir and Harlaw. The former covers more than 2,000 acres in area, the latter some 300, their capacity totalling around 700 million gallons. Used nowadays only for compensation purposes – to maintain levels in the Water of Leith, River Almond, and Union Canal – they are part of a water-supply network which was one of the first municipal systems in the United Kingdom, and which is described more fully under Fairmilehead.

BLACKHALL

*Government: (local) split between wards 6 (Davidson's Mains)
and 8 (Craigleith).
(national): Edinburgh West. Community council designated,
but not formed.*

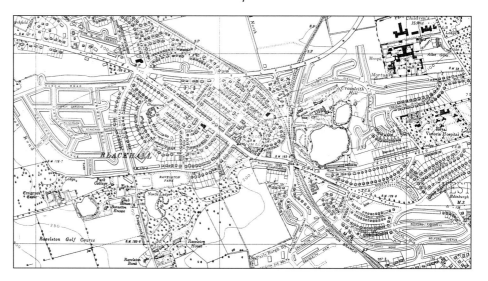

Nowadays Blackhall and nearby Craigleith fully fit the description of a suburb, being characterised by the *Statistical Account* for their 'stretches of raw red roofs', which have mushroomed in the area. Of the two, Blackhall has the longer history as a community, while Craigleith was distinguished, quite literally, for being a hole in the ground.

Blackhall began as a linear village along the Queensferry Road, probably in the first half of the 19th century, local historian Margaret McArthur pointing out that no maps appear to carry any mention of a settlement here before 1773. She theorises that the name 'Blackhall' may comprise a sanitised version of 'Clarty Hole' – not an unlikely theory for an area which encompassed two quarries within its immediate area. Nearer to the village was Maidencraig quarry, mined from around 1628 to supply building operations at Edinburgh Castle, and later the North Bridge. Flooded by the middle of the 19th century, Maidencraig is now a housing development just yards from what became Blackhall's main street. But Maidencraig was not the clartiest hole in the area. That distinction belonged to Craigleith.

Until as recently as the mid-20th century, Craigleith quarry was Edinburgh's deepest and most impressive. First excavated in 1616, the open workings here produced a cliff 200ft deep as men toiled to produce pale orange stone from the Lower Carboniferous for such key Edinburgh buildings as the castle and 'Scotland's Disgrace' on the Calton Hill. It seems to have reached its fullest depth and extent between the wars of the 20th century, but today has vanished entirely

– no doubt much to the relief of local parents – and in 1995 was replaced by the kind of extensive retail park more readily associated with the outskirts.

With the loss of its railway station, the district has become part of the homogenous spread of bungalows all the way from Ravelston to Barnton. Yet Blackhall still has a thriving primary school, although dwarfed by the arrival of Mary Erskine's merchant school from Queen Street in the 1970s.

Further reading:
Bunyan, I.T. *Building Stones of Edinburgh* Edinburgh Geological Society, 1987.
McArthur, Margaret *Blackhall past and present* Roxburgh Publications, 2000.

BROUGHTON

Origin of name: from Anglian 'broc tun', meaning 'farm beside the burn'.
Government: (local) Broughton ward, shares community council with New Town and Pilrig;
(national) Edinburgh North and Leith constituencies.

Broughton was regarded in 1792 as the northern outpost of the city, according to the parish minister, who doubtless was able to look down the slope to Canonmills on the river, and Leith in the distance. Notorious for its witches and warlocks, Broughton is now an amorphous area to the east and north-east of the New Town, running as far eastwards as Leith Walk. No signs remain in this heavily built-up area of its past supernatural connections, nor of its pastoral nature.

Edinburgh's first zoo was created here in 1839, at Broughton Park. It lasted until the mid-1850s, seemingly forced to close when the animals died from stress caused by the fireworks displays promoted by the park to celebrate the ending of the Crimean War. Not only did the city's zoo have its origins here, but the present Royal Botanic Garden, presently on its fourth site, 'rested' in Broughton for over 60 years on its way from Canongate to Inverleith. The site on the west side of Leith Walk comprised five acres, including a pond and a 140ft-long greenhouse. All this was dwarfed somewhat by the 75 acres which became available at

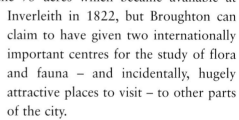

Inverleith in 1822, but Broughton can claim to have given two internationally important centres for the study of flora and fauna – and incidentally, hugely attractive places to visit – to other parts of the city.

The main thoroughfare of the immediate area is Broughton Street, although it is shorter than it once was. At one time its southern end met Leith Street approximately where the north-east end of John Lewis's store is now, meaning that St Mary's Metropolitan Cathedral had Broughton Street as its postal address. This, one of Britain's smaller cathedrals, is separated from a new entertainment and hotel complex by the city's most extensive roundabout, and certainly earns its adjective of 'metropolitan'. The seat of the Archbishop of Edinburgh and St Andrews, St

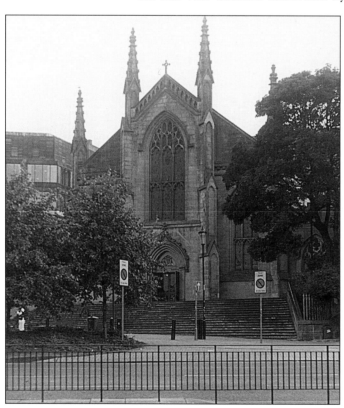

Broughton Street once stretched farther south than it does now, taking a direct line towards the north-east corner of what is now John Lewis's store in Leith Street. In that short length it incorporated two major buildings, the only one of which to survive is St Mary's Metropolitan Cathedral. The seat of the Archbishop of Edinburgh and St Andrews, this is the principal place of worship for Edinburgh's Roman Catholics. Edinburgh's only other cathedral is St Mary's Episcopalian in Palmerston Place (see Haymarket). St Giles's, being a Presbyterian centre of worship, does not of course rate as a cathedral.

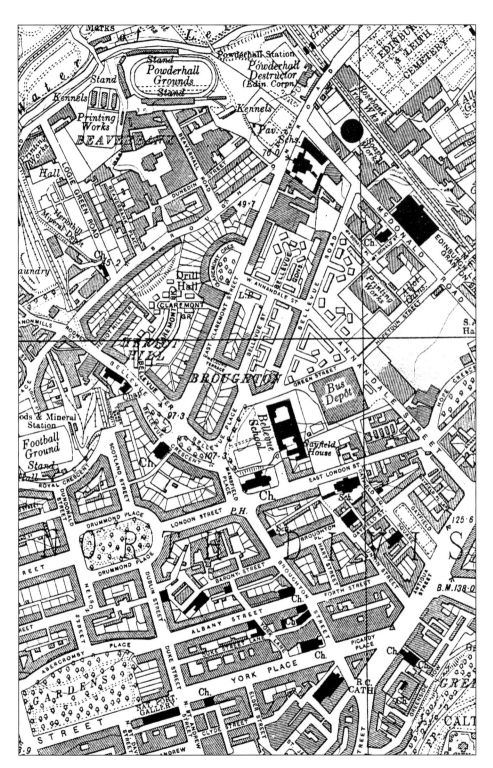

Mary's Metropolitan lacks a spire to mark its existence to the visitor, although it is an important focus for Roman Catholics in central Edinburgh.

The new Warner Village opposite St Mary's inherits a strong tradition of entertainment from the building some 50 yards down Leith Street. Although not

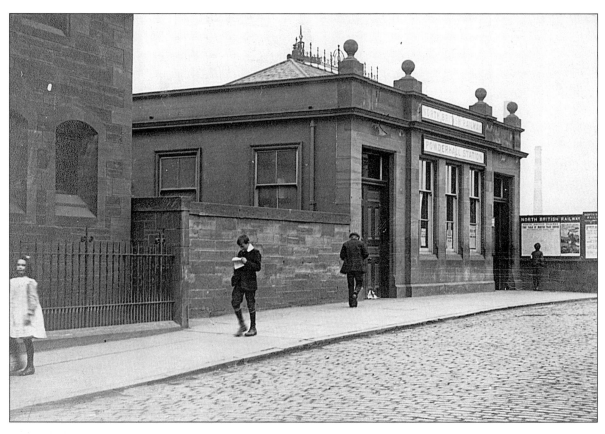

At one time Edinburgh had around 50 railway stations, but it is now down to one-tenth of that number. Shown here is Powderhall station, situated in Broughton Road, located between the present-day whereabouts of the new refuse compactor and Redbraes Park. The station closed in 1917 and the building has now vanished, but a glance over the wall will show the passer-by that the line beneath, which now terminates here instead of going on to Leith Citadel and Granton as it once did, is used by trains carrying compacted refuse to local landfill sites. (Edinburgh City Libraries)

strictly situated in Broughton, the Playhouse Theatre was the largest cinema in Edinburgh when it opened in 1929, although the 3,000-seat auditorium showed its last film in 1987, and stage shows now rule here. Just down from the Playhouse was the Salon, a popular 'second run' cinema, which no older resident can recall showing anything but westerns.

The Picardy Place roundabout is decorated by some impressive sculptures – none more so than the work of Leith's Sir Eduardo Paolozzi on its south side – but a more conventional statue just north of the roundabout, almost hidden in a glorified car park and loading bay, should not be ignored. For this is none other than Sherlock Holmes, deputising for his creator, Sir Arthur Conan Doyle, who was doubtless considered less likely to be recognised by motorists negotiating Britain's most competitive roundabout.

Conan Doyle was born at a site facing the top of Broughton Street in 1859, and although he qualified in medicine at the city's university, found that his pen could support him comfortably. Edinburgh references are few and far between in his work, but are interesting enough when they do appear. Salisbury Crags rates a mention in Conan Doyle's novel *The Lost World* as a model for the sheer walls of the Matto Grasso, but it was an Edinburgh professor, Joseph Bell, who was to provide the prototype for Conan Doyle's master creation, Sherlock Holmes. Apparently, Bell's use of deductive logic and interest in the arcane fascinated the young medical student, who in turn presented him to a reading public which has

never tired of him yet. Not only did Holmes make Doyle the only late-19th century British writer who could rival Dickens in popularity, but both creator and created still feature prominently in present-day television drama.

Broughton school opened in 1909 but has now moved to the Fettes area, and a huge industrial hall was built here in the 1920s, hosting exhibitions and boxing matches before becoming the city's largest bus garage. The Broughton area also had its own market, whose walled location can still surprise anyone coming across the site – just off Dublin Street – by accident. Like Stockbridge, this was a 19th-century market established to contest the traditional monopoly of trade held by the Town Council. Nowadays, it is a haunt of advertising executives and small business-owners, but with a little landscaping – flower tubs, ivy, heritage lighting – could be a unique part of the city, particularly since its Stockbridge counterpart is now reduced to little more than an archway.

Just up Dublin Street from here is the birthplace of Sir Nigel Gresley. The house itself carries no commemoration, and it has to be said that Edinburgh has made little of a locomotive engineer who, although he died over 60 years ago, is still revered throughout the world of transport. Gresley designed steam locomotives which combined power with celerity, and such engines as the *Flying Scotsman* and the *Mallard* are household names. The latter achieved the highest accredited speed – 126mph – of any steam locomotive anywhere, and if this seems routine in today's world of diesel and electric traction, the reader has to imagine the *Mallard*'s heavy piston rods having to withstand the stress of revolving eight times a second.

Broughton Place runs at right angles off Broughton Road, seen in the foreground, still with its tramlines in this 1951 picture. At the far end of the place can be seen Broughton Place Church, built in 1820-1, described by the Penguin Buildings of Scotland as 'unusually pretentious for a Secession Church', complete with Greek Doric portico. (Edinburgh City Libraries)

Broughton still has a self-contained market, seen here from its western entrance in Dublin Street. This is an interesting area, although some redevelopment is presently proposed, which will hopefully preserve the character of the site, which is more substantial than that of Edinburgh's other 'independent' market, that of Stockbridge.

The southern part of Broughton looks over the Water of Leith to Warriston. On this bank, much has changed. Until recently, Powderhall stadium stood here, hosting greyhound racing and giving its name to the famous New Year Sprint. This was an event years ahead of its time – it was open to professional athletes. Housing now occupies the site here.

Another loss is the Duncan chocolate factory, which could be depended upon to declare its existence to all and sundry through their olfactory, if not their alimentary, systems! (In other words, you didn't have to buy a Duncan's hazelnut bar to know how good it was!) Unfortunately, the company received a financial incentive to move to the west of Scotland at the end of the 1980s, leaving local people to ponder why the local enterprise company could not have secured this important industry for Edinburgh, where it had made its name, and where local employees put their savings on the line to secure the company's future when threatened by closure.

A less attractive, but no less important, addition to the Broughton skyline is the city's main refuse disposal unit. Comprising an incinerator and compacting equipment, the Powderhall site deals with refuse from up to a quarter of a million homes and businesses. Much of the material is loaded into rail vehicles for landfill disposal, currently in Midlothian. There is apparently no legal requirement on Scottish local authorities to recycle even a proportion of waste, although this would appear to be the desired future for refuse disposal.

CANONGATE

*Origin of name: 'Way of the Canons' (ecclesiastical).
Government: (local) ward 34 Holyrood;
(national) Edinburgh Central. Community council designated
but not formed.*

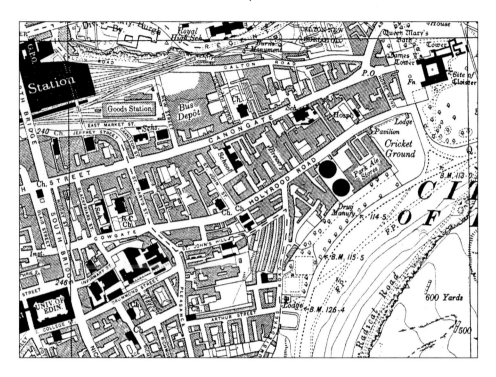

As late as the 1960s, it was not unusual to hear Canongate folk talk about 'going up to Edinburgh' – even though this constituted a journey of only a matter of yards! Now normally thought of as that part of the Royal Mile below the Netherbow crossroads down to Holyrood, Canongate was in fact a burgh quite separate from Edinburgh, although very much under its domination, until 1856. Technically, Canongate was a royal burgh, having been the product of a royal gift from David I to the Augustinian canons of Holyrood. Unusually, the ecclesiastics decided to surrender their right to appoint baillies in favour of the burgh residents – an early example of devolved government highly appropriate to a parish that includes the new Scottish Parliament!

Holyrood Abbey is the most eminent building in Canongate. Dating from 1128, when it was established by David I following an encounter with a stag whose antlers had entrapped a holy rood (or cross), the abbey, and its Augustinian builders, had to endure a tumultuous history. Having been built outside the city walls, the abbey was poorly protected from pillagers from south of the border. The enemy scarcely cared that Holyrood was based on the design of Merton Abbey in Surrey, but further research into the abbey's early building has been

Holyrood Palace from the Abbey Strand at the foot of the Royal Mile. Unlike Buckingham Palace, Holyrood is a royal residence which sits cheek-by-jowl with the sovereign's subjects. It is rumoured not to be one of HM's favourites, although she will surely regard that the construction of the new Scottish Parliament just yards away as an improvement on the brewing premises there previously.

frustrated, not just by invaders' damage, but because so many archives concerning its construction have been lost.

After the final English pillage in 1547, James V decided to establish a residence here, although the site was not completely secularised until the beginning of the 17th century. This transitional period was particularly stormy; the Stewarts' attempts to establish a Catholic chapel here not being well received by the Canongate parishioners, who used their new place of worship, Canongate Kirk, opposite Moray House, as their parish church. In 1688, in fact, the Catholic chapel at Holyrood was badly damaged, and some of the tombs of the Scottish kings desecrated.

The palatial aspect of Holyrood was much diminished by the departure of James VI's court to London in 1603. His son Charles I paid a historic visit in 1633, but Cromwell later stabled his horses here, and much of the damage done then was not made good until the Duke of York (James VII) made it his base for six years from 1679. The palace then had to wait for the arrival of Queen Victoria and her Prince Consort before major refurbishments took place, with Prince Albert creating Dunsapie and St Margaret's lochs to ensure a good water supply. Nowadays many of the furnishings are believed to be 'pooled' in the royal inventory, and have no particular attachment to Holyrood. Nevertheless, the palace's connection with Mary Stewart (Queen of Scots) is sufficient to guarantee its popularity with countless visitors, for many of whom the highlight of the visit is to see the room where the wretched David Rizzio was stabbed to death in front of the queen.

The older Holyrood Abbey became a ruin, the roofless building apparently inspiring Mendelssohn to write his *Scottish Symphony* in 1829. Attempts to reroof the shell have proved to be a failure, and no major attempt at restoration appears to have been undertaken since 1945.

Holyrood's court was the matrix for dancing and theatre in Scotland, two forms of entertainment which have spread through the city centre and into other suburbs. Formal dancing was a regular feature of court life, with less glorified mortals enjoying dancing at weddings and on the comparatively few holidays available to them. Both theatre and dancing were frowned upon from time to time by religious authorities, and actively legislated against by their municipal counterparts. It was in the 20th century, with increased leisure time available, that Edinburgh really put on its dancing shoes, and suburban ballrooms flourished away from the more central Assembly Rooms in George Street. Tollcross and Fountainbridge boasted the Cavendish and Palais, while Leith had its own

Queen Mary's Bath still stands on the edge of Holyrood Palace grounds, just down from Abbeymount. This 1860 photograph shows that it was once part of a residential area of Canongate, belying its palatial appointment. Current historical thinking suggests that the 'bath' building was in fact some kind of summer house or lodge. (Edinburgh City Libraries)

Assembly Rooms (and Eldorado Ballroom), and Morningside its Plaza. The largest ballroom of all was to be found at the Marine Gardens at Portobello. Nowadays, not one of these still operates as a venue for formal dancing, although the Cavendish is now a night club.

Canongate boasted its own tolbooth (extant, and not to be assumed as Edinburgh's, whose tolbooth, a hybrid of erstwhile town hall and prison, no longer stands beside St Giles). The People's Story Museum here specialises in working-class history, while Moray House opposite is the main municipal museum for Edinburgh (the better-known Royal Museum and Museum of

Scotland are of course national establishments).

Canongate's kirkyard, just off the High Street, rivals Greyfriars in historical importance, and is almost as well known as the kirk itself, with its distinctive appearance. Facing the High Street is an unusual circular window, while the cruciform building contains galleries once reserved for the magistrates and officials of this once-independent burgh. Former ministers include the late Reverend Selby Wright, a well-loved parish minister who cared deeply for his community, and reached out to those outside it with his blessings of those brave and active enough to accompany him at daybreak on May morning to the windiest corner of his parish – the summit of Arthur's Seat. Probably the graveyard's most famous interment was that of Robert Fergusson, the ill-starred poet whom Burns revered as his mentor, and to whom he dedicated a gravestone. James Craig, architect of Edinburgh's New Town, is also buried here, back in the Old Town which he did so much to consign to history.

The Canongate enjoyed its own police, banking, and theatres, often in advance of the city itself, but in 1856 an amalgamation took place with Edinburgh which was perhaps long overdue. By this time the number of Canongate constables stood at 20 volunteers, who were not popular with local people because of the assistance they rendered naval press-gangs. In fact, exactly 100 years before, a constable was accidentally 'pressed' off to sea, the remaining constables at that time resigning their commissions in protest at the city's failure to force the Admiralty to return their colleague.

As for theatre, Canongate appears to have pioneered custom-built drama venues in the capital with the opening of the Concert Hall at the head of the Canongate in 1747. It was here that John Home's play *Douglas* was premiered –

Edinburgh's nickname of 'Auld Reekie' (or 'Old Rocky', as rendered in a recent video commentary about the city) is easily understood in this historic photograph dating from 1896. From this Calton Hill viewpoint much of Canongate can be seen, with Queen's Park and the lower slopes of Salisbury Crags to the left. (Edinburgh City Libraries)

One of the most interesting smaller mansions in the city is to be found in the St Leonard's area, on the boundary between Canongate and Newington. This is Hermits and Termits, a house constructed in 1734 for an excise official. In the following century it found itself at the gates of the city's first railway coal yard, with coals being brought here under Samson's Ribs by railway tunnel, but the area is once more largely residential and the building a pleasant anomaly amid newer construction.

this being the drama which so excited a member of the audience that he shouted out 'Whaurs yer Shakespeare noo?' Modern audiences are less enamoured with the play, and each revival of Home's work is greeted with incredulity that it could ever have prompted such enthusiasm.

One curious aspect of Canongate housing commented upon in the *Third Statistical Account* was that it replicated all the worst characteristics of the dwellings higher up the slope in Edinburgh. Here, there was just as much in the way of precarious tenement construction as west of St Mary's Street, yet the *Account's* contributor argues that Canongate was not constricted by city walls as Edinburgh was. This however overlooks the fact that the burgh was bounded on the north side by the Nor' Loch and by an open sewer running eastwards, while the royal park has always presented a barrier to the east.

Few communities have exported so many people and survived as a viable entity. Comparing the 1951 and 1961 census figures shows that, in the 1950s, Canongate's population declined by nearly one-third, with little in the way of new housing taking the place of the now-redundant tenements, as their inhabitants moved to the new schemes on the periphery of the city. Nowadays, however, there has been considerable residential development south of the Cowgate through Dumbiedykes and up to St Leonards.

Although an area of intensive – and, all too often, slum – housing, the Canongate did include one important little patch of green. This was the Physic Garden, created by the university in 1670. Originally occupying a mere 40sq ft at St Anne' Yards near Holyrood, the garden, specialising in medicinal plants and herbs, was moved to a one-acre site where the Waverley station is now (see the plaque opposite platform 11). This garden was unfortunately damaged in the siege of 1689, at which time there were believed to be 2,700 plants. In the 18th century, the garden moved yet again, to Broughton, and finally to Inverleith.

Brewing is no longer carried out in the area, the Holyrood brewery having closed in 1986. This had inherited the Canongate's brewing tradition which went back to the abbots of Holyrood Abbey who brewed from the 12th century. A modern brand-name made its appearance here six centuries later when William Younger arrived to take advantage of the area's natural springs. Closure of the S & N plant in 1986 left a site which was selected unexpectedly for the new Scottish Parliament, although this has led to the demolition of a fine Victorian office building. Another successor to a former brewing property is the Dynamic Earth, a £15 million tourist attraction opened in 1999, bringing the science of geology to life. Not an inappropriate site in which to do this, with the birthplace of James Hutton, known as the 'founder of modern geology' just up the road at St Leonard's, and with the remains of an extinct volcano brooding above!

Hutton is a good example of a prophet without honour in his own country. The city has no major statue to him, although he was painted by Henry Raeburn in his lifetime, and the chair of Geology at Edinburgh University is named for him. But, since Hutton was to geology what Darwin is to zoology, perhaps he deserves more than this. His achievement was to realise that geology is a long-term process moulding the planet on which we live, and that a Biblical timescale was never going to be sufficient to explain how our landscape evolved.

Hutton published his conclusions in 1788 under the title *The Theory of the Earth*, but, like Darwin in the next century, met with a barrage of opposition from both the religious and scientific communities. In particular, the 'Neptunic' theories of Gottleib Werner, effectively based on belief in Noah's flood, held sway throughout Europe and in Edinburgh itself. Here, Leith-born William Jameson embraced Wernerian philosophy wholeheartedly, and succeeded in turning out more Wernerian students from Edinburgh University than Werner himself. Meanwhile, Hutton, never a professional academic, was less able to promote his beliefs, and even now is less well-known to the present-day citizen than the other members of the city's great quartet of scientists and thinkers – Napier, Hume, and Clerk Maxwell.

Another 'export' from the Canongate is Hibernian FC. The club was originally formed at a Catholic Boys Club in St Mary's Street, but its history is discussed under Leith, a community it is more usually associated with. The same Canongate street also used to be the site of the Star Cinema, and its story sums up the intensive nature of communal life which has now deserted the Canongate. According to cinema historian Janet McBain, writing in her book *Pictures Past*, the Star's management appeared to fight a losing battle against local children determined to enter the cinema without paying – this despite the fact that an empty jam jar was often sufficient payment to gain entry. Not surprisingly perhaps, the picture house failed to prosper!

CANONMILLS

Origin of name: from mills established by canons of Holyrood.
Government: (local) wards 17 (Stockbridge)
and 19 (Broughton);
(national) Edinburgh North and Leith. Covered by Stockbridge
and New Town/Pilrig/Broughton community councils.

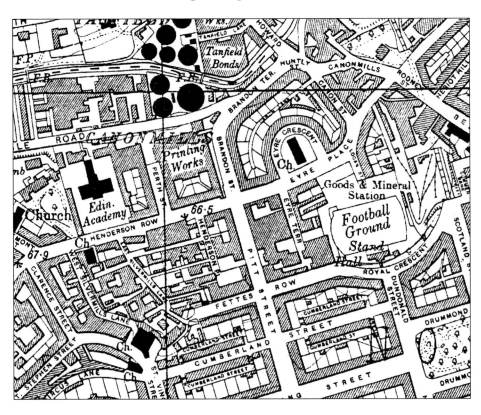

Edinburgh Academy is just off Henderson Row in Canonmills, the product of parents' dissatisfaction with the Royal High School in the 1820s. Sir Walter Scott and Lord Cockburn were among those instrumental in having the rival school established and a handsome building by William Burn resulted. The most famous 'old boy' was undoubtedly James Clerk Maxwell, the physicist later hailed by Albert Einstein as his intellectual predecessor, and, among other things, producer of the first colour photograph.

Occupying the Water of Leith valley immediately east of Stockbridge, Canonmills, as the name suggests, was a corn milling settlement worked by the monks of Holyrood from the 12th century. The playground and small industrial estate just off Eyre Place occupy the site of Canonmills, where one of Edinburgh's

lochs used to attract anglers from far and wide intent on catching pike and perch. The city's first curling club first met here in around 1750, but the loch was drained in the 1840s, part of the site becoming Scotland Street railway station, connecting by tunnel with the Waverley (the bore still exists, running southwards under Scotland Street and St Andrew's Square). A funfair called the Royal Gymnasium took up residence here and the level piece of ground immediately south of Eyre Place was later the venue for St Bernard's football club.

Edinburgh Academy is located here, on the border with Stockbridge. Established in 1824, the academy was the result of the dissatisfaction felt by many Edinburgh luminaries, including Sir Walter Scott and Lord Cockburn, with the High School, the standards of which were perceived to be in decline at that time. Probably the academy's most famous pupil was to be James Clerk Maxwell (1831–79), the ground-breaking physicist and producer of the world's first colour photograph.

Canonmills can boast one of Edinburgh finest examples of 'colony' houses, a series of terraces abutting the Water of Leith. Built on a co-operative basis over a 50-year period up to 1911, they have become particularly popular with young first-time buyers in preference to a tenement flat. Nearby is Glenogle Baths, completed with a 75 x 35ft pool in 1900.

Film buffs still recall Dame Maggie Smith cycling in Henderson Row as the cameras recorded her performance of Miss Jean Brodie for posterity. The same thoroughfare used to house a power station for the city's cable cars, and a representative vestige of winding gear is preserved at the doors of a new insurance building.

Canonmills was once associated in the public mind, particularly in the 19th century, with entertainment. In April 1865 a fairground was opened immediately south of Eyre Place, and west of Scotland Street railway station, known as the Royal Patent Gymnasium. Owned by Robert Cox, later MP for Edinburgh South, its main feature was the 'Great Sea Serpent', described as a rotary boat seating 600, and presumably the feature at the centre of this contemporary photograph. Robert Louis Stevenson used to come here for the torchlit skating when the water was frozen, and, along with his friends, delighted in the advertisement for 'café au lait, with or without milk'. (Edinburgh City Libraries)

From almost the same spot where the picture of the 'Great Sea Serpent' was taken, (next page) the cameraman could have turned and taken an 1860s view of Scotland Street which would looked much like today's, apart from the change in street lighting and the inevitable cars. Although close to Canonmills, Scotland Street is built on a higher level – after all, Canonmills was once almost entirely a loch – and this is really the northern part of Edinburgh's New Town. At least the residents no longer have to listen for the rumble of trains under their feet, the tunnel connecting Waverley station and Scotland Street station having closed to passengers in the 1860s.

Canonmills is very much characterised by such edifices, the townscape being transformed in recent years by the opening of the striking Standard Life building next to Tanfield Hall. (The insurance industry's contribution to Edinburgh's townscape is discussed in more detail under Newington). Tanfield is a pleasant mix of old and new, the hall having been the site of the declaration of the Free Kirk in 1843 – as recorded by artist David Octavius Hill (using photography to aid his brush), later becoming the city's principal site for boxing matches, a sport in which Edinburgh can easily outrival Glasgow.

Henderson Row is the principal east-west thoroughfare in Canonmills, with its western end in Stockbridge and its eastern now transformed by modern buildings produced by companies working in the financial sector. East of here Canonmills loch was once to be found, later replaced by a fairground and railway station, and later still by a sports ground. This is a community which has never quite made up its mind whether it is a residential or industrial area.

COLINTON

Origin of name: believed a transliteration of a charter for land owned by Colgan family.
Government: (local) ward 43 (Colinton);
(national) Edinburgh Pentlands. Entitled to community council but none presently formed.

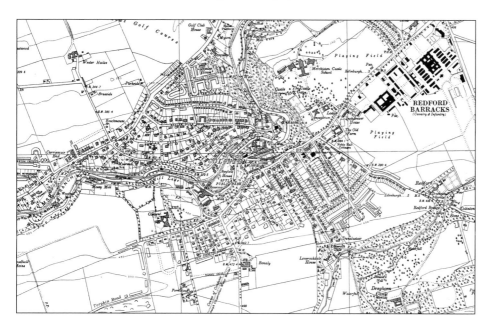

Listed in the *First Statistical Account* as 'Collington', Colinton was originally a self-contained village community in 'Edinburghshire', as Midlothian was long known. Writing in 1794, the local minister recorded that only 300 people had lived in the vicinity some 90 years before, but, with 1,395 living in the parish at the time he was writing, 'this is a very great degree of population, compared to the extent of land' (5,070 acres). Perhaps not what we would look on as overcrowded by present-day standards!

Even in the 18th century, the power of the Water of Leith was being harnessed. No fewer than 71 mills operated along a 10-mile stretch of the river near Colinton, 14 of them producing flour, 14 milling corn and 12 barley. Snuff was also produced in five mills and paper in four.

A rail connection with Edinburgh from 1874 allowed access to the city's West End in only 14 minutes, so it was no surprise that Colinton was formally absorbed into the capital in 1920, although it still retains much of its pastoral charm. With passenger trains withdrawn in 1943, however, journeys into the city by public transport now take longer!

Redford barracks was established near here in 1915, resulting in the village holding the unexpected distinction of becoming one of the first localities in

Colinton tram terminus on a rainy winter's day in 1946. A tram which has arrived on the number nine service from Granton is being prepared for the return journey by the simple expedient of having its power connection – its 'pole' - realigned from one end of the vehicle to the other. The village of Colinton became part of the city of Edinburgh in 1920 and was connected by tram service within another six years. This was sufficient to see off the rival rail service to Princes Street station; this failed to survive the war years, and the trams themselves gave to way to buses in Colinton in October 1955. (Edinburgh City Libraries)

Scotland to be bombed from the air, by Zeppelin *L22* in April of the following year. No one was killed, the village being spared the carnage caused by the attack on Edinburgh and Leith on the same evening. The heavily censored newspapers of the time, in revealing that a village 'in south-east Scotland' had been attacked from the air, treated this disparagingly as proof that the Germans were unable to master basic navigation. In fact, the target appears to have been the new Redford barracks, and *L22*'s sister, *L14*, attacked both the Castle and what its crew thought were barracks in the Haymarket area (actually Donaldson's Hospital). In reality, the civic authorities in both Edinburgh and Colinton had no means of defending their communities against air attack, or even of warning the inhabitants by lowering and raising gas pressure (for domestic lighting) as a signal, as practised by many English local authorities. Colinton escaped lightly.

While it may have been 'outside' Edinburgh until the 1920s, nevertheless Colinton has played a part in the essential supply of water to the growing city. Torduff and Clubbiedean reservoirs are within walking distance of Colinton, while the Bonaly utility, higher in the Pentlands, is now effectively a nature reserve. Torduff is the reservoir closest to Edinburgh. All of 72ft deep, it had a capacity of 110 million gallons, and was completed as early as 1818.

Bonaly Tower itself is a house with a fascinating history. It was built by and for the Cockburn family by William Adam, and is most frequently associated with Henry, Lord Cockburn, the high court judge whose *Memorials of his Time* is one of the best examples of 19th-century historical testimony to be found in English

Just off Bridge Road in Colinton is Spylaw Street, named after James Gillespie's estate nearby. Gillespie, who established the school of the name, made his fortune in snuff manufacture, using power from the nearby Water of Leith.

literature. Another literary figure associated with Bonaly was the novelist Evelyn Waugh, who attended an officers' training course here during World War Two and was delighted to find his family's coat of arms displayed on the staircase. His family was related to the Cockburns, a fact which, Waugh commented, gave him little pleasure, as he would have preferred to have descended from a completely useless lord. His diaries record, interestingly, that he found Scottish army officers far superior to English ones, his course commander Alec Buchanan-Smith (later Lord Balerno) being a perfect illustration of this superior mettle.

Spylaw Park makes a pleasant centrepiece for this lovely part of Edinburgh, and the former railway is now converted to a footpath beside the river which gave so much vigour to community life in the former village of Colinton.

The Water of Leith, seen here looking eastward from Colinton's bridge, is a 22-mile river wending its way from the Pentlands to Leith. Now relieved of its industrial responsibilities – there were once 70 mills on its course, and ships were launched into its higher tides at Leith – it is now an important wildlife corridor. Otters and kingfishers are among the river's inhabitants, and it is no longer tidal at its mouth.

CORSTORPHINE

Origin of name: possibly Gaelic; 'Crois Torfin', or 'Torfin's crossing' of Gogar loch. More romantically, although less likely, perhaps a semantic record of the donation to the parish church of a gold cross by a noble French visitor, thus 'Croix d'or, fine'. Government: (local) wards 13 (East Craigs), 14 (North-east) and 24 (South-east Corstorphine) and 23 (Gyle); (national) Edinburgh West. Community council.

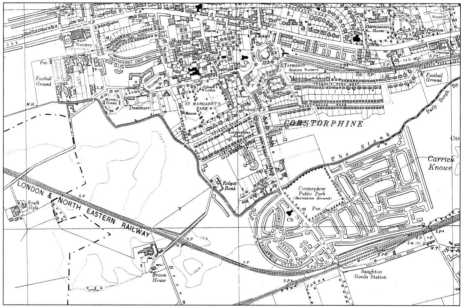

Corstorphine no longer has its castle, built by the Forrester family, but the doocot has survived the parent building's demolition. More than 1,000 pigeons were kept here at one time, although not for reasons of animal welfare – this was a simple form of husbandry, supplying fresh meat to its owners throughout the winter. The beehive-style structure, taller than the street lamp nearby, is now in the care of Historic Scotland.

Like Colinton, Corstorphine is a Midlothian village which has been swallowed up by Edinburgh. Housing to the north, halfway up the slopes of Corstorphine Hill, and to the east and west, has completely enveloped what was once an independent community.

Corstorphine was originally situated just to the north of the isthmus between Corstorphine and Gogar Lochs. Both of these are now drained, the local aristocratic family, the Lords Forrester, no longer bringing their provisions from Edinburgh 'by water carriage, in a boat, from Coltbridge' as the parish minister put it in 1793.

The village was a one-street community which was a farming centre for its surrounding area. Dung from the city streets was used as a fertiliser in preference to lime, but the area was not fully drained before 1800. Forty years later, the parish minister observed, in the *Second Statistical Account*, 'notwithstanding its proximity to Edinburgh... it is only in comparatively recent times that Corstorphine has been brought generally into cultivation'.

By the second half of the 19th century, market gardening had developed to supply the burgeoning city to the east, and the railway arrived nearby in 1842 (although the first Corstorphine station was some distance to the south, at Saughton). Corstorphine, absorbed by Edinburgh in 1920, rapidly became an attractive suburb for commuters, particularly with the city's west end only 11 minutes away by train, although the area attracts visitors in its own right, with Edinburgh's zoo established here during World War One. The Forestry Commission offices are a newer arrival, and the former village now finds a huge retail and business development growing at South Gyle to the south-west.

The most interesting building in Corstorphine, just a few yards from the end of the High Street, is the Old Parish Church. There has been a religious establishment on this site since 1426, although the present building is a collegiate extension to a larger place of worship no longer extant. One architectural writer has criticised the uneven roofline as evidence of poor building practice, but the building nevertheless has a compact and pleasing appearance, even to the passing atheist. (Ian Taylor)

Corstorphine High Street is no longer the main thoroughfare in the former village; that dubious honour belongs to St John's Road, the main Edinburgh-Glasgow trunk road. But the old street is still an important link between the south-west of the city and the new retail establishments near the Drum Brae roundabout, so much so that there seems little likelihood of Corstorphine High Street being pedestrianised as has happened in Balerno. This Saturday morning view is looking westwards, with a stream of traffic heading for the new supermarket just down the road.

The branch railway line (opened 1902) closed inexplicably in 1969, sentencing the locals to nearly 15 years of continual traffic congestion, now slightly eased by the long overdue building of the city bypass.

Corstorphine is famous for the Scottish National Zoological Park, or Edinburgh Zoo for short. Considered among the top three in the United Kingdom, the capital's zoo was opened on the south side of Corstorphine Hill in 1915 and is now one of Scotland's leading tourist attractions, as well as an internationally recognised centre for species conservation and zoological science in general. The opening of the zoo was somewhat rushed, the newly arrived animals being ushered into enclosures not yet ready for them. One brown bear had no difficulty in scooping soft cement out of the floor of its cage, and was soon discovered by the zoo's director, Tom Gillespie, sharing cream buns with an elderly lady! She was full of praise for the management who allowed the animals such freedom, while Mr Gillespie, showing admirable calmness, persuaded her to bring her food into a nearby cage, leave it on the floor for the bear following eagerly behind, and hotfoot it to the gate!

The zoo is particularly noted for its penguin collection, the largest in captivity in Europe, although captivity is perhaps not an entirely accurate description for birds which are allowed to parade through the grounds once a day. It's not so long ago, in fact, that they could seen proceeding along the pavements beside the A8, but the traffic is too noisy for them now. Interestingly, the gardens were established with the help of funds made available from the closure of the city's first zoo, at Broughton.

As well as hosting the zoo, the 531ft high Corstorphine Hill features an area of parkland topped with Clermiston Tower. Designated as a local nature reserve,

the local wildlife, believed to include a number of protected species not found elsewhere in the city, is not helped by the local authority's determination to use the site for firework displays in perverse contradiction of the spirit of nature conservation.

Another reminder of Corstorphine's history – in a community careless enough to lose its castle – is the Dower House. Once part of the castle complex, this is of 1660s construction and recently restored. Situated just off the former High Street, this is now a local history centre and a pleasing reminder both externally, and in its exhibits inside, that this was a thriving village independent of Edinburgh until only about 80 years ago.

CRAIGLOCKHART

Origin of name: 'crag once held by the Lockhart family'.
Government: (local) ward 26 (Craiglockhart);
(national) Edinburgh Pentlands. Community council.

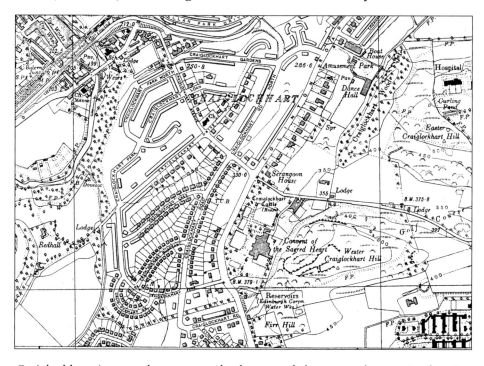

Craiglockhart is a south-western suburb, one of the most pleasant in the city, lying to the north of the twin peaks of Craiglockhart hill. Mainly commuter country, it holds an unusual place in World War One history, as its military hospital (now part of Napier University) housed Siegfried Sassoon and the

Displaying festival pennants from its trolley rope for the last time, a tram on the number nine service approaches Craiglockhart railway station from the Colinton direction. Its destination on this day, 3 September 1955, was Granton, but buses took over the route only seven weeks later, on 22 October. Behind the fence in the background was another transport medium, the Union Canal. (W.S. Sellar)

doomed Wilfred Owen during their convalescence from injuries received at the Western Front. Their story was translated from Pat Barker's novel *Regeneration* on to the silver screen, although with a west of Scotland college substituted for Craiglockhart.

The two hills here are Wester Craiglockhart (575ft) and Easter Craiglockhart (519ft), bisected by the road running to Morningside. Like the Castle Rock and Blackford, the wester hill represents a geological formation known as 'Crag and Tail' formation, with the volcanic rump facing west, and the diminished tail sloping to the east. The hills include in their flora purple milk vetch and maiden pink, with dog's mercury and common dog violet found in the neighbouring woodland. This slopes down to what used to be the site of the former Happy Valley leisure complex, now Scotland's top venue for tennis and badminton. Here there are eight outdoor and six indoor courts, with total seating capacity for 2,000 spectators. The pond here is a haven for swans and ducks, but as late as the 1930s was the city's premier outdoor skating rink in winter, complete with floodlights.

To many older residents, Craiglockhart is synonymous with 'Happy Valley', a sports and leisure complex just off the Colinton Road. Its successor is the Craiglockhart Tennis and Sports Centre, opened in 1994 to offer the highest standard of tennis and badminton to all comers. In the foreground is the pond which was once rated as the best outdoor ice-skating venue in the city, and was even floodlit at night. Now the coots, swans and ducks have it to themselves, and there is a nature trail nearby, established by local people who wished to boost the area's natural history potential.

CRAIGMILLAR

Origin of name: from early British meaning 'the brow of a hill'.
Government: (local) ward 57 (Craigmillar);
(national) Edinburgh East and Musselburgh. Community council.

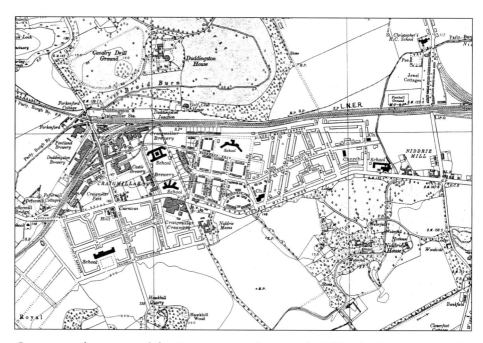

Craigmillar Castle is one of Edinburgh's most interesting historic sites – one which is comparatively unknown to visitors from outside Scotland and underestimated by those who live here. The stronghold of the Preston family, the castle was sacked by the Earl of Hertford during the 'Rough Wooing' in the 16th century, but was viable enough as a stronghold for Mary Stewart, Queen of Scots, to receive the English ambassador here in the 1560s. Now in the care of Historic Scotland, the structure overlooks the suburb which has grown up on its north side, and the new Royal Infirmary to the south.

Once a rural area noted for its cream produce, and within the last 50 years the location of one of Britain's biggest brewing centres, Craigmillar is now essentially a residential area. Situated south-east of the city centre and south of Portobello, Craigmillar has a population of between 15,000 and 20,000, almost entirely accommodated in council housing. Unemployment is worse here than anywhere else in the city, with the social problems and vandalism that often follow in its wake, since the closure of the coal mines, breweries and an ice-cream factory.

One industry which survives is biscuit-making, in the Peffermill area. The factory here specialises in ice-cream biscuits, and is heir to a long industrial tradition.

Niddrie Mains Road echoed to the sounds of the demolition crews just round the corner when this picture was taken in the winter of 2002. Much, if not all, of the 1930s housing is due for demolition and replacement by more compact houses with their own front doors, a considerable improvement on the tenement-style houses which were built before. Nor have local people waited for outsiders to help them improve their environment, as the establishment of the Craigmillar Festival Society proves. This group not only set in motion a regular programme of social and cultural activities, but extended its scope into giving practical assistance to those in need.

Leith was the first area to produce biscuits in quantity – since they were easier to store and consume on long voyages than bread – but the city built up a reputation for producing some of Scotland's finest biscuits. Unfortunately, the brand names of Crawford's, McVitie Price and Mackies are now either defunct or operating away from the capital.

The area has a royal pedigree, centering on Craigmillar Castle, brooding on its hill to the south-west of the present-day community. Preserved nowadays by Historic Scotland, it was originally built by the Preston family in the 15th century, and comprises an L-shaped tower within inner and outer courtyards. Although

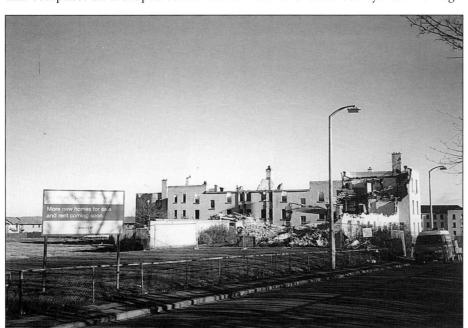

Craigmillar had more shops and churches than such later schemes as Muirhouse, Pilton and Wester Hailes. There was a cinema, the Rio, with an art deco façade. Much of the industry has closed, including all seven local breweries, an ice-cream factory and two coal mines within a mile or two. Employment can be found at the biscuit factory and in retail developments at Peffermill and on the outskirts of Newcraighall.

The Jack Kane Centre, just off Niddrie Mains Road, is one of Craigmillar's most important buildings. Its grimly windowless appearance belies its recreational function, almost giving the impression of a prison block. It was designed by the City Architect's Department in the mid-1970s and named for a popular Lord Provost who declined to accept the knighthood which was then an automatic reward for the Edinburgh's civic head.

This is one of Edinburgh's lesser-known watercourses, the Niddrie Burn, seen here running northwards through Craigmillar. Rising near Swanston, this is known as the Lothian, Burdiehouse, and Niddrie Burn before becoming the Brunstane Burn and flowing into the Forth on the city's eastern boundary, between Eastfield and Musselburgh.

damaged (like Lauriston) in the 'Rough Wooing' of 1544, it was sufficiently rebuilt by Sir Simon Preston for Mary Stewart, Queen of Scots, to be a frequent caller, and here she once received the English ambassador. Probably appropriately called 'Edinburgh's second castle', this is a historical gem all too often ignored by Edinburgh people, never mind tourists.

In 1964 a group of Craigmillar residents led by Helen Crummy decided to take positive action to improve their environment and their communal lifestyle. By forming the Craigmillar Festival Society, they set in train a series of local events which stretched beyond the festival that was the centrepiece of their plan. The society has a permanent office and undertakes community activities all the year round, and is staffed by volunteers and social work trainees.

More recently a £300 million rehousing programme has been launched, leading to a improvement in living conditions locally. The natural environment has not been forgotten, with Scottish Natural Heritage involved in tree planting, landscape design and environmental clean-ups, some of them on the Niddrie Burn (Braid Burn).

However, Craigmillar has lost both its railway station (shared with Duddingston) and its cinema. The Rio or County, known colloquially as the 'Gamp', showed its last film in 1963, and was demolished as recently as 1997, after latterly offering bingo as its only attraction. The branch library thrives and, like its counterpart at Wester Hailes, appears to be one of the best stocked in the city.

60

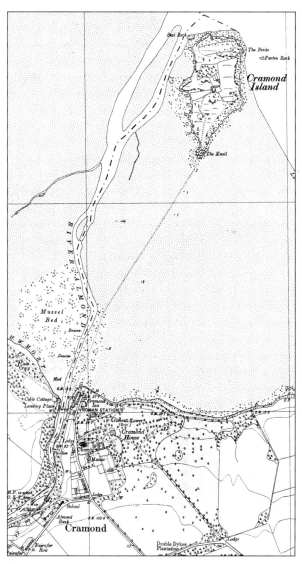

CRAMOND

Origin of name: from early British meaning 'fortified place on the Almond'.
Government: (local) ward 5 (Cramond);
(national) Edinburgh West.
Community council designated but not formed.

Recent excavations suggest that the Romans built a fort at the mouth of the Almond as far back as AD 142, but the present-day community at Cramond has made little of what, for many others, would be a powerful tourist attraction to exploit. Cramond villagers obviously believe that their community is attractive enough as it is, and they would be difficult to argue with on that score. Perhaps the recent discovery, in the mud of the Almond, of an impressive leonine statue, has stimulated more local pride in the village's Roman past, and new excavations, complete with interpretation facilities, have begun.

The whitewashed, red-roofed cottages make up one of Edinburgh's most beautiful areas, yet the village was a hive of industry in the 18th and early 19th centuries. The *First Statistical Account*

Sunset at Cramond, c.1980. Nowadays this view has changed and will almost certainly include the sight of massive oil tankers loading at Hound Point, near South Queensferry. Nevertheless, Cramond retains its charm as one of Edinburgh's most attractive and popular suburbs.

Donkey race at Cramond around the dawn of the 20th century. Judging by the uniform and respectable appearance of the boy 'jockeys', this was probably a school outing to the village and its sands, but further details are lacking. (Edinburgh City Libraries)

The fashions may appear Edwardian, but the style of ferry transport at Cramond is unchanged, and this photograph could almost have been taken this year. Those crossing the Almond in this way – propelled by a single oar – are probably going to walk part or all of the way to Dalmeny. The Almond was designated as the western boundary of Edinburgh in 1603, although this was moved westwards to include South Queensferry in 1975. (Edinburgh City Libraries)

Cramond in the early 1930s. Reading the First *and* Second Statistical Accounts *provides a completely unexpected view of Cramond as an industrial centre producing iron goods, particularly nails, and trading directly with ports in the Baltic, as well as oyster harvesting. This fascinating village has a history which goes back to the second century of Roman rule in Britain, but which had settled down to a more genteel lifestyle by the time this photograph was taken.* (Edinburgh City Libraries)

Cramond parish church dates from 1656 although built on the site of an older mediaeval place of worship, which in turn was probably built on Roman remains. Immediately to the north of here is the main exposure of the Roman establishment here, so the whole site is steeped in history. The church was extensively altered in the 19th century, although the original tower remains relatively untouched.

of the parish, compiled in the 1790s, portrays an almost unrecognisable industrial community of some 300 people, the tiny port providing a base for no fewer than seven sloops voyaging to and from the Baltic to import crude iron for conversion to steel in the riparian mills of Cramond. These produced iron implements, from nails to anchors, but water power from the river proved to be too unreliable to make Cramond competitive in the increasingly industrialised world, particularly since coal had to be brought specially to the area, principally from Bo'ness. By the time the *Second Statistical Account* came to be written in 1845, Cadell's ironworks were listed as one of only two 'manufactures', the other being paper production, although 100 villagers were employed at that time.

A longer-lasting occupation was oyster fishing, but even that has now vanished, leaving Cramond as a highly desirable residential area. Nowadays, its residents may well be the most prosperous in the city; no less than three-fifths of

the houses contain six or more rooms, three times the city average. Car owning statistics show that Cramond has 1.37 cars per family (city average 0.69), with nearly five percent of Cramond motorists owning three or more cars each.

CURRIE

Origin of name: possibly Gaelic topographical term for a boggy plain or river bank.
Government: (local) ward 2 (Baberton); (national) Edinburgh Pentlands.
Community council.

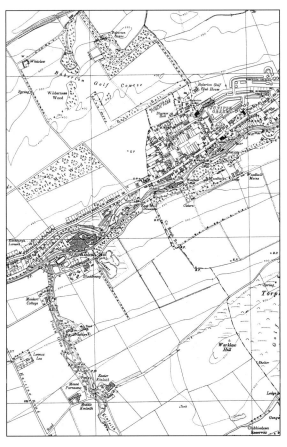

Situated between Juniper Green and Balerno, Currie has much in common with both of them; a riverside village that once had a number of mills based on the Water of Leith, but with a modern suburbanite population enjoying the fresh air of this former Midlothian community.

Writing in the *First Statistical Account* in 1792, the parish minister remarked on the longevity of the inhabitants of Currie, one of his parishioners living to be 113 years old, and working as a labourer almost up to his death. Another local farmer was still working while a mere 105. Not surprisingly, the minister described his parishioners as 'sober, industrious, and economical', although 'the vices of the capital however are beginning to spread fast among them'. He named the drinking of tea as one of the 'vices'!

Along with Balerno and Juniper Green, Currie was originally one of three villages west of Edinburgh along the Lanark road; in fact the parish of Currie included both of the other two. The Water of Leith provided power for milling or producing snuff and paper, and the coming of the railway in the 1880s encouraged commuter traffic to and from Edinburgh. A station had also existed on the mainline since around 1850. The three villages were all absorbed by the city in 1920. This 1900 view shows the old kirk and village school. (Edinburgh City Libraries)

The modern community takes the form of housing grouped along the main Lanark road. Although the area lost its passenger railway station on the Balerno branch in 1943, services to both Edinburgh and Glasgow are available from nearby Curriehill station, reopened in 1987 after a 36-year hiatus (*O si sic omnes!*). Heriot-Watt University has created its modern campus in the Currie area, at Riccarton. Currie RFC play their Division One rugby at Malleny Park, almost to reinforce their village's suzerainty over Balerno next door, although this means a shorter walk for sports fans living in the latter village.

South of Currie is Juniper Green, a riverine community once a village in its own right in the Water of Leith valley. Supposedly named after a natural colony of junipers, the village grew from virtually nothing at the end of the 18th century to become the largest of the four along the river by the beginning of the 20th. The river powered a number of mills here, with snuff being produced from 1749 until the 1940s, along with agricultural milling and some light industry.

The coming of the railway in 1874 made Juniper Green popular as a pleasant dormitory for the city, and the area is now very much suburbanised, the railway track a riverside walkway. This attractive suburb, absorbed with Colinton by the city in 1920, scarcely deserves the twice-repeated assertion in the *Third Statistical Account* that Juniper Green has 'no ancient character of its own, and with nothing of historical importance to show'.

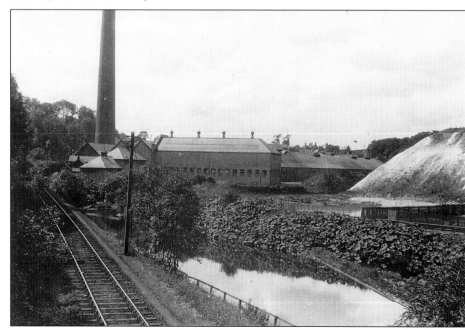

DALRY

Origin of name: possible Celtic, British or Gaelic derivations, all topographical.
Government: (local) ward 30;
(national) Edinburgh Central. Shares community council with Gorgie.

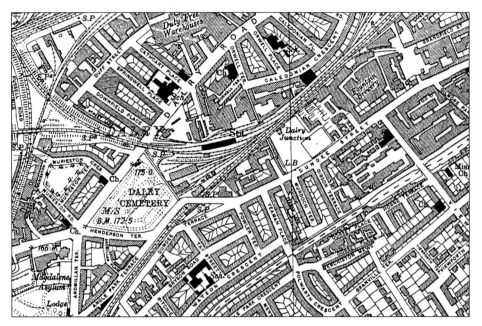

South-west of Haymarket is an intensively populated area, known as Dalry, after the burn which once drained the Burgh Loch to the Water of Leith. Nearly all the housing here dates from the second half of the 19th century, and consists almost invariably of tenements, although there are some 'colony' houses near the Haymarket end of the district, and 'model' housing, dating from 1855, just off Fountainbridge.

Historians interested in the area benefit from a carefully-researched text written and published by Malcolm Cant, and the interested reader can do no better than to read his work (see Bibliography). The almost pastoral state of Dalry is recorded there, with Dalry House (extant) as the only major residence. Originally home to the Chieslie family, one of whose members was executed for murdering the Lord President over a litigation decision, Dalry House was taken over by the Brand family, who attempted to have the area renamed Brandsfield. The new title failed to last, and the coming Industrial Revolution transformed the area beyond all recognition.

Railway depots and yards once provided much employment here, as did breweries, although both industries have now greatly reduced their presence (the Fountain Brewery is still active – see Tollcross). The Union Canal, having lost its

Dalry Road looking eastwards. This is the A71, heading on to Kilmarnock through Gorgie. On the right of the picture is one of the city's best-known cemeteries; little surprise that the pub just up the road to the right, although officially the Athletic Arms, is popularly known as the 'Diggers', and is reputed to serve a rare pint. The bridge in the background of this shot carries part of the Western Approach Road between Lothian Road and Murrayfield; here it follows the course of the branch line from Princes Street station to Leith North. Dalry Road had its own station, with its entrance just beyond the bridge.

passenger and freight traffic to rail, took on the role of a water conduit for Dalry's rubber mills until 1967, when the factory moved out to Midlothian to take advantage of a governmental assistance scheme. Needless to say, Edinburgh was denied access to the scheme – despite its chronic unemployment problem – and the observer is tempted to speculate that politics had more than a little to do with it. When a Labour government established a selective area assistance scheme in the 1960s, Edinburgh was firmly Conservative in its local politics. Curiously, the city failed to benefit from the scheme, losing rubber, printing, and crystal-making to Labour Midlothian, all within a few years. When Labour finally took control of the City Chambers in 1988, a Conservative government at Westminster had torn up all regional aid schemes! Thus Dalry lost its Castle Mills in 1967, 4,400 employees moving off the 22-acre site, as the industry left for Newbridge.

Leisure and learning have instead become important parts of the Dalry experience. In 1937 work began building what was to become an Art Deco public library in Dundee Street; it was not completed until March 1940, when war had darkened the skies over Edinburgh. The building also incorporates the Nelson Hall, used for talks and recitals, and the Scottish Book Centre, which promotes reading for all. The building and its literary contents represent an impressive addition to the landscape; imagine your author's surprise therefore when he was recently denied access to the library on the grounds that it was *Tuesday*! Let us hope that this misplaced spirit of economy is only temporary.

A new feature for Dalry is the UGC cinema and leisure complex at Fountain Park, its many attractions including an Imax screen, Edinburgh's first. A cinema on a smaller scale is the Friday afternoon picture show at St Bride's community centre in Orwell Terrace. Local residents can enjoy a deliciously vintage film for a mere 60p at the time of writing! Of course, St Bride's is more than just a weekly cinema, offering concerts, keep-fit and dance sessions, as well as providing one of the city's best-known Fringe venues.

To the west, the area merges with Gorgie at the foot of Henderson Terrace, where traffic lights at green cheerfully usher opposing streams of vehicles into one another's path (watch from a safe distance, or retire to the 'Diggers' – officially, the Athletic Arms – to ponder the highway planner's arts).

Symbolising the durability of Dalry as a community, Dalry House has been restored to its 17th-century glory, and fulfils an important community function as a day centre for the elderly. A modern architectural guide describes it as 'overwhelmed by tenements', but what else could you expect in such an intensively inhabited area?

DAVIDSON'S MAINS

*Government: (local) wards 5 (Cramond), 6 (Davidson's Mains)
and 7 (Muirhouse);
(national) Edinburgh West. No community councils.*

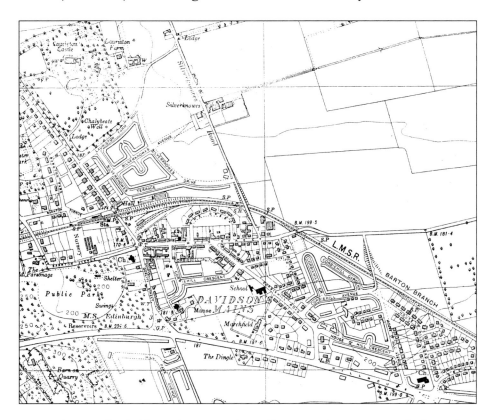

Situated virtually halfway between the affluence of Barnton and the urban landscape of Muirhouse is Davidson's Mains, although its citizens can claim that their community is older than either. Once known as Muttonhole, the village became Davidson's Mains in around 1850, the name being taken from the Davidson family who owned the mansion of Muirhouse in nearby Marine Drive. The village's annual gala reinforces the message that this is no mere suburb of Edinburgh, although the spread of bungalows to the north suggests otherwise, and the area now has many daily visitors to its supermarket.

A popular residential suburb to the south of Cramond, Barnton is essentially a post-war addition to the cityscape, one transport historian pointing out that major development began in earnest here as soon as the railway link with Princes Street was closed in 1951! It was as if its inaccessibility to the general public was its greatest perceived attraction for the better off (although the Queensferry Road is not far away). Barnton is one of the more affluent suburbs of Edinburgh, sharing with Cramond the highest proportion of multi-roomed houses, and of three-plus car ownership, for the whole of the city.

Golf is an important part of Barnton's landscape. In 1895–7, the Edinburgh Burgess Golfing Society and Bruntsfield Links Golf Club took up residence here following a sojourn at Musselburgh, after their course in the Meadows area had became too cramped (and despite having the venerable Golf Tavern – extant – as their clubhouse). Lack of space is not now such a problem, although one American visitor to the Barnton course, which commands a view of the Forth to the north, was heard to ask if 'the pond' was part of the course!

Lauriston Castle is a fascinating feature to the north. This is one of the city's most interesting museums, but there can be few other museums which can date their existence to the 16th century, or claim that they were sacked by the Earl of Hertford during the 'Rough Wooing' of 1544. Major rebuilding was obviously necessary once the English were finished with it, but by the 1590s Lauriston had become a family home, being taken over by Archibald Napier, father of the inventor of logarithms (and more usually associated with Merchiston). By the end of the following century, ownership has passed to John Law, Comptroller-General of France, and one of history's first international financiers. Following a succession of owners, Lauriston was gifted to the city, complete with a fine collection of antiques, by the Reid family in 1926. Set in 30 acres of parkland, frequently used for rallies and children's events, Lauriston Castle is one Edinburgh's finest attractions.

East of Davidson's Mains is Muirhouse. Along with Pilton, Muirhouse was the biggest council housing development of the 1950s, creating a huge residential scheme in the north-west of the city from 1953 onwards. It suffered from the usual thoughtless urban planning, which combined the city's largest concentration of two and three-room houses with a serious lack of communal and shopping facilities (the shopping centre was not built until 1971). A recent TV feature on urban deprivation alighted on Muirhouse much as the 1930s newspapers might have featured Glasgow's Gorbals. The reduction in the gas industry nearby has worsened employment prospects here, although a local initiative scheme is currently doing its best to improve opportunities for residents in the area.

Davidson's Mains is still recognisable as a village community, this shot showing Main Street looking eastwards. Just off to the right is Quality Street, believed by some to have inspired the title of the play by J.M. Barrie, which in turn found its way on to a confectionery box. In fact, North Berwick also has a claim, as did Leith at the time that Barrie was writing. In this volume Davidson's Mains is 'book-ended' by the differing communities of Barnton to the west and Muirhouse to the east.

DUDDINGSTON

Origin of name: from estate owned by Dodin de Berwic in early 12th century.
Government: (local) ward 58;
(national) Edinburgh East and Musselburgh.
Northfield/Willowbrae community council.

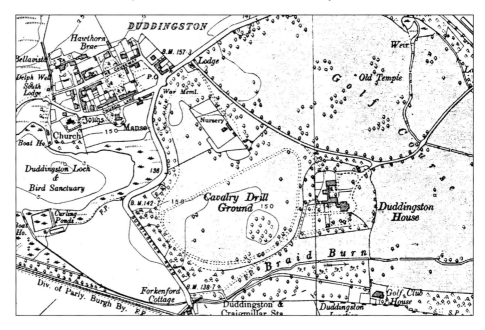

A linear village at the south-eastern entrance to the Queen's Park, (although the parish extended to Easter Duddingston, nowadays Joppa), Duddingston is one of the oldest inhabited parts of Edinburgh. The earliest inhabitants were lake dwellers living in stilt-supported crannogs, but the terrestrial village grew from the siting of the kirk, founded in the 12th century and still characterised by a fine Norman arch.

The description of Duddingston in the 1792 *Statistical Account* reads strangely nowadays, with the parish minister describing the local industries of brickmaking from the local claybeds (in present-day Craigentinny), the 13 seams of coal found locally – drained by square-boilered steam engines – and the saltpans at Magdalene Bridge (on

Duddingston's kirk nestles on its outcrop overlooking the loch, as seen from the southern slopes of Arthur's Seat. The church retains parts built by the Normans in the 12th century, although it underwent a considerable rebuilding in 1889. Beyond the loch, a bird sanctuary since the 1920s, can be seen the apartment buildings of Craigmillar.

Not all skaters on Duddingston loch were as famous as David Wilkie's subject the Revd Robert Walker, whose image was transferred from canvas to postage stamp a few years back. In this (probably Edwardian) picture, local youths are venturing out on to ice where nowadays all but the birds are banned, as the loch is now, quite rightly, a bird sanctuary. (Edinburgh City Libraries)

the coast between Eastfield and Fisherrow). The antiquity of the parish probably explains its extent, some eight square miles in area, running from Arthur's Seat to the sea, across much of what is now East Edinburgh.

Although most of the buildings in present-day Duddingston date from the 19th century, the village was part of the Holyrood debtors' sanctuary at one time, and it was here that James Tytler edited the second edition of the *Encyclopaedia Britannica*. A penniless polymath, Tytler took over the editorship of what was to become the most important reference work in the English language, working for only a few shillings a week, after the editor of the first edition, William Smellie, turned down the challenge of increasing the original number of volumes from three to ten. Tytler's remuneration was a pittance considering his work on both the second and third editions, the latter, based almost entirely on his labours, making his publishers a profit of some £42,000.

Duddingston was where Sir Henry Raeburn pictured the skating minister of the Canongate, an image reproduced some 150 years later on a postage stamp. Skating was popular here until the loch was declared a bird reserve in the 1920s, and it is now administered by the Scottish Wildlife Trust.

Duddingston is the location of Edinburgh's oldest pub, the Sheep Heid Inn, possibly established as early as the 14th century. The pub's name comes from the gory habit of hill farmers slaughtering their animals on the lower slopes of Arthur's Seat, but sending the cadavers citywards without the heads. The latter were sold to the locals, to be boiled or baked, the practice commemorated in the name of this excellent pub. Although this is not the original building, it is still well worth visiting.

Arthur's Seat, Edinburgh's principal hill, broods over Duddingston, although it could equally be described under Canongate or Abbeyhill, so close is it to the

Even in the depths of winter, Duddingston can still look worthy of a picture postcard. Here the Norman kirk is seen from the south with the Queen's Drive very prominent halfway up Arthur's Seat. The loch is in the foreground of this picture, although invisible because of the growth of reeds. Not surprisingly, bittern have been known to visit Edinburgh's most important bird sanctuary.

city's heart. All of 822ft in height, it constitutes the principal remains of a volcano active 354 million years ago (plus or minus another seven million, according to the geologists). It is believed to have been underwater when it first became active, the resulting eruption propelling the cone upwards and opening five vents, all but one in the present-day Queen's Park (the exception being the Castle Rock).

The hill can be climbed from most directions, although an approach from Duddingston allows the use of 'Jacob's Ladder', an open-air staircase as far up as Dunsapie Loch. Even from here the view is impressive, and the less fit can reach this spot by car from the Piershill entry near St Margaret's Loch. From here the summit can be reached easily by the able-bodied, and a return via Duddingston at least justifies a call at the Sheeps Heid!

Not the Highlands, but a winter view of Dunsapie Loch, just above Duddingston, and part of the Queen's Park landscaped by Victoria's consort, Prince Albert. A lone jogger is being splashed by wind-driven spray from the loch, with the camera lens being similarly affected.

FAIRMILEHEAD

Origin of name: modern usage dates from 1780s, but earlier origin is disputed (see Bibliography under 'Harris').
Government: (local) wards 44 (Firhill) and 52 (Fairmilehead); (national) Edinburgh Pentlands. Community councils in both Fairmilehead and Firrhill.

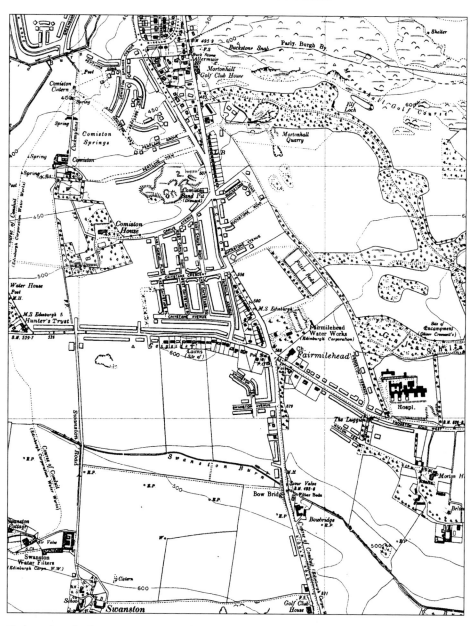

Robert Louis Stevenson wrote that at Fairmilehead you could still hear 'the cry of the curlew'. Nowadays that noise would be drowned out by the roar of traffic on, heading for, or from, the A720 city bypass at Lothianburn roundabout.

Not many British cities are overlooked by ski-lift and chair-lift, but Edinburgh is! These facilities give a glorious view northwards, past Arthur's Seat and Salisbury Crags to the Firth of Forth. The bungalows of Fairmilehead are well to the fore in this picture, as is the Princess Margaret Rose orthopaedic hospital on the middle right. The A720 bypass is not obtrusive in this photograph although its roar is continuously present to walkers a thousand feet above on the Pentland ridge.

Fairmilehead as viewed from just above the upper works of the ski and chair lifts at Hillend. These facilities originally belonged to the city of Edinburgh, but are now 'relocated' to Midlothian. Although sited at the bottom of the lifts, the Inn on the Hill was Edinburgh's highest pub, but is now unfortunately closed.

Nevertheless, this book's author recently saw waxwings here, so Fairmilehead's pastoral status is not totally degraded.

With most motorway traffic from the south reaching Edinburgh off the A702, Fairmilehead has become the principal gateway to the city for English visitors. (If you doubt this, observe the coach traffic coming up for the Tattoo every August!). Comparatively recent in origin, the community here is almost entirely residential. Bungalows stretch in all four directions from the crossroads where the A702 meets Oxgangs Road running west, with Frogston Road West heading off eastwards. The church situated at the north-east corner here is a landmark familiar to commuters from the south (and, no doubt, Tattoo-goers). Completed in 1937, it is characterised by a Dutch-style entrance tower. Despite the newness of this suburb, there is a robust sense of community here, with a community council being formed for the first time in 2001.

If Fairmilehead has an industry, it has to be water which comes to mind. For some years this was the headquarters of Eastern Scottish Water, and the old water boards before it, based around filtration beds which are screened from the main road by trees, but are very prominent to the walker looking down from Hillend. There are two supply points for the city here, four at nearby Firrhill, with others at Alnwickhill (Liberton), Torduff and Hillend.

This area has played a crucial part in the history of Edinburgh's water supply. It was the Comiston Springs, at Oxgangs Avenue just south of the present Braidburn Valley Park, that were first piped in 1676 for three miles to a supply reservoir at Castlehill, filling five (later 14) street wells in the Old Town with a desperately needed continuous supply. Over the decades, the parched city sent its engineers southwards, diverting and utilising supplies from ever farther away, culminating in the massive reservoirs of Talla and Megget, the latter opening in 1983. This has led to the 'liberation' of the original Comiston supply, now acting as a natural compensator for the Braid Burn.

Another part of the area with a fascinating history is Swanston. Separated from the rest of Edinburgh by the new bypass, Swanston village shelters under the Pentland Hills, and is forever associated with Robert Louis Stevenson. The village itself consists of eight white-washed 19th-century cottages, which must be among the few in southern Scotland to be thatched (with reeds from the Tay). Water was piped from here to Castlehill early in the 18th century, to supplement the first piped supply from Comiston, and a 'water house' still survives here. The village was well restored by the local authority in 1964 and is one of the city's most attractive locations, although the lack of a focal point may disappoint some visitors. Stevenson summered here from 1867 to 1880, the village featuring in his novel *St Ives*.

The Pentland hills to the south form the city's landward

Edinburgh as seen from the Braid Hills, between Morningside and Fairmilehead. The viewfinder in the foreground was installed in 1995, the day of its unveiling by the Lord Provost being almost the only occasion in that long hot summer when it actually rained!

Hunter's Tryst dates from 1939. Nowadays there is a busy roundabout here, with the main thoroughfare, Oxgangs Road, connecting the Oxgangs estate with Fairmilehead crossroads, while the opening to the left takes the shopper to a busy superstore. (Edinburgh City Libraries)

Oxgangs, to the west of Fairmilehead, contains 'Edinburgh's best collection of 1950s architecture', according to author-architect Charles McKean, and this shot of Comiston Mains Church shows a building which dates from only 1954, its design showing traditional Scottish values of harling and a substantial square tower.

boundary, although the actual Edinburgh/Midlothian border is immediately south of the A720 bypass, so it is Midlothian's hills which loom over the capital from the south. Until local government reorganisation, Edinburgh was able to boast of being the first local authority to install an artificial ski run, and this facility, now administered by Midlothian Council, can still claim to be the UK's longest. It is complete with ski and chair lifts, although 'après ski' facilities have been somewhat reduced with the closure of what used to be Edinburgh's highest pub, the Inn on the Hill.

West of Fairmilehead, Oxgangs sprawls southwards from the slopes of Craiglockhart Hill towards the green belt. A council house development begun

by the city council in 1954, Oxgangs has, unlike some such schemes, good community facilities, but there is little local employment, making good public transport so much more of a necessity.

GILMERTON

*Origin of name: believed to signify farm belonging
to Gilmour family.*
*Government: (local) wards 55 (Moredun) and 56 (Gilmerton);
(national) Edinburgh South. No community council.*

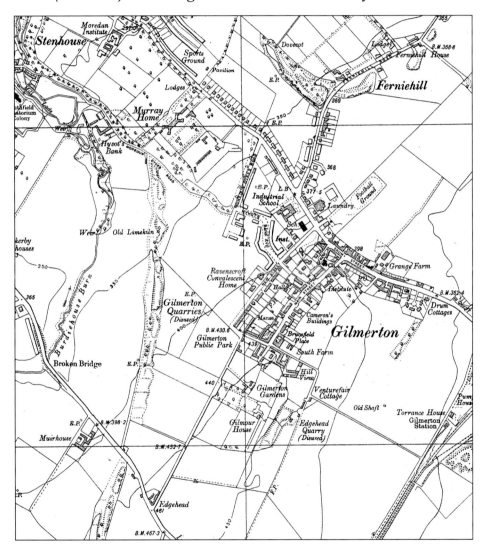

Despite having its origins as a community back in the 12th century, located within
the parish of Liberton, present-day Gilmerton has been almost swallowed up in
the great swathe of new housing on the southern outskirts of the city. Its past
industries were partly agricultural – an annual Carters Play was held – and partly
based on coal mining. No fewer than 20 seams of coal were exposed here in the
1780s, although only a quarter were then being worked. The last mine closed in
1961. Thirty-five men were employed at a local limeworks in 1786, producing
70,000 bolls of lime annually for agricultural fertiliser.

Gilmerton is now incorporated into the city's suburbs, but has a strong tradition as an independent community. Its culture was horse-based, with its carter's ceremony, so it is highly appropriate to include this shot of the 'Gilmerton Lad' Clydesdale horse and proud owner, pictured in July 1933. A description of Gilmerton published only seven years previously primly expressed the hope that 'morals and manners, have, it may be hoped, vastly improved at Gilmerton...'
(Edinburgh City Libraries)

The most interesting antiquity in the area is Gilmerton Cove, a series of underground chambers believed to have been hewn in the early 18th century (although probably on the site of an earlier work). It contains living and storage chambers, but its purpose and precise function are unclear.

To the east of Gilmerton Road is the intriguingly-named Little France, so called, it is believed, because of the number of French-born courtiers and artisans who lived here while serving at Holyrood. This is now the site of the new Royal Infirmary, moved from the area beside the Meadows since 1870. (See also Marchmont). The infirmary was established by public subscription organised by Lord Provost George Drummond in 1725. Gilmerton is in fact its third location, the first building having been situated in Robertson's Close, later rebuilt as Infirmary Street, where only five beds were available initially, occupied for an average of five weeks per patient. A custom-built infirmary building was constructed in 1738–48, designed by William Adam. Demolished in 1884 after the hospital moved to Lauriston, the 'second' infirmary is shown in archival photographs to have been an architectural gem, although both the building, and the site it stood on, were undoubtedly too small for the purpose. So it is in its Lauriston location that Edinburgh citizens think of 'their' infirmary, although

Gilmerton crossroads, seen here pictured in Edwardian times. To the visitor, the local feature with most interest is Gilmerton Cove, an underground construction completed in 1724. Its 'builder', or more correctly, burrower, was local blacksmith George Paterson, and he and his family proceeded to live there for the next 11 years. (Edinburgh City Libraries)

how much ownership the public will exercise over the new Gilmerton utility remains to be seen, given the PFI element in its construction.

Edinburgh citizens tend not to associate Gilmerton with air travel, but it was at a site in this vicinity that 77 Squadron of the Royal Flying Corps set up a temporary airfield following the Zeppelin raid of 1916 (for more, see Leith). The *Third Statistical Account* records that in 1935 the city of Edinburgh purchased land in the Gilmerton area for the construction of a civic airport, but soon realised that the size of the site required had been underestimated. Apparently the city had experienced obfuscation in its dealings with the Air Ministry at the time – just as the Leith Dock Commissioners did when attempting to give Leith an airport.

A photographic record of the Gilmerton brass band around the dawn of the 20th century. Written sources on Gilmerton are surprisingly hard to find, and the Statistical Accounts have been judgmental on a community which, despite its proximity to the city, had an agricultural flavour to its lifestyle, while also supplying manpower for the lime and coal extraction industries in the central Lothians. (Edinburgh City Libraries)

GORGIE

Origin of name: from British 'gor gyn' meaning upper wedge of land. Pronounced with both gs hard.
Government: (local) ward 29 (Shandon); (national) Edinburgh Central. Shares community council with Dalry.

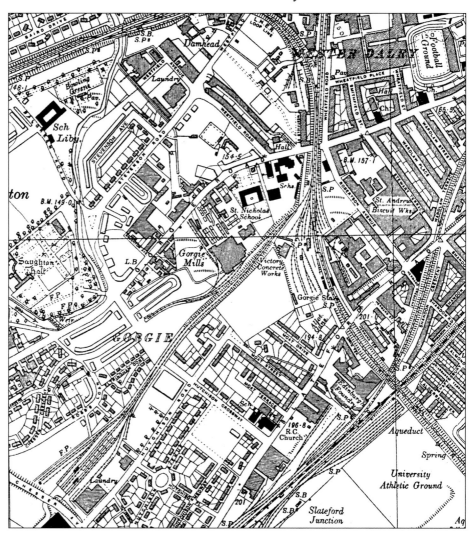

Like Dalry to the east, this is an industrious area, which accommodated the city's slaughterhouses from 1911, as well as breweries, railway and tram depots, and latterly a huge telephone exchange. Nearly all of this has now vanished, although an electronics factory and brewery compensate.

The City Farm was established just off Gorgie Road in 1982, and is run as an educational charity. While a highly popular visitor attraction, the farm is hardly representative of the present day's agricultural industry. Its location in Gorgie is not inappropriate however; it is easy nowadays to underestimate the former importance of the Gorgie meat markets, once a major employer in the area. With much of their area now given over to housing, the city has received a long-term benefit in the conversion of the Cornmarket building into a concert venue.

Another local industry is brewing, the Caledonian Brewery in Slateford Road dating from 1869. This was established by the Lorimer family and was later taken over by Vaux, but was the subject of a management buy-out in 1987. The new concern is prospering – despite two fires in the 1990s, one of which destroyed one of the three original copper vessels used to boil the hops. This has been largely replaced, and the 'Caley' has now outlasted the Vaux company which was so determined to close it down, despite its excellent record of continuous production.

From time to time, proposals are produced for the reopening of Edinburgh's suburban railway, and Gorgie is perhaps a good starting point for discussing this one-time means of getting around Edinburgh's suburbs. Gorgie (or more exactly, Gorgie East) was the first station on the line for inner-circle trains, that is, those leaving Waverley and Haymarket, and then heading round the south of the city before returning to Waverley through Portobello. Outer circle trains made the opposite journey, and until 1952, many of the services worked in and out of Leith Central station, thus linking the heart of Leith with the likes of Craigmillar, Morningside and of course Gorgie. This was an invaluable service for workers – the author made his last trip on an inner-circle train in 1960, meeting his father from his work at Blackford Hill and accompanying him home to Portobello. This journey unfortunately took longer than it needed to as the diesel-powered trains were operated on schedules designed for steam services! There were no services at all after the evening rush-hour, so the line's potential was never really developed. The line is still intact, although freight is now the only traffic, apart from an occasional diverted passenger train. There is presently no electric catenary.

Football is an important part of Gorgie's history. Despite spasmodic attempts by the club to move out into the green belt, Gorgie is still the home of Heart of Midlothian FC, at Tynecastle Park, wedged between Gorgie Road and Tynecastle Secondary School. Formed in 1876, Hearts supposedly took their name from a Cowgate dance-hall, and not the stone emblem among the High Street setts where the former city tolbooth used to stand. Adopting maroon as its colours from the start, Hearts FC were Scottish champions twice before World War One began in 1914, and that momentous event proved to have a traumatic effect on the club. The entire first team volunteered for military service, joining the 16th Battalion of the Royal Scots. Seven players failed to return, two more managed to continue their careers despite having been gassed. A memorial to their sacrifice can be seen at Haymarket crossroads.

Like Hibs, Hearts enjoyed their best years in the 15 or so after World War Two, when their attacking 'Terrible Trio' of Conn, Bauld and Wardhaugh provided a

high degree of footballing entertainment, rewarded with two league championships, the Scottish Cup in 1956, and two League Cups. The European Cup was competed for twice, and on merit each time (Hibs, in contrast, made their one and only entry in Europe's top tournament by invitation). In the last 20 years Hearts have defeated such well-known continental opposition as Bayern Munich, Dukla Prague and Sparta Prague in competitive matches at home, although the team's away form in Europe has always let it down.

Under Leith will be found a brief history of Hibernian FC, so it is only appropriate to discuss 'derby' matches between the two clubs here – from the Hearts point of view, of course! While Hibs can probably claim to have enjoyed the more spectacular wins in recent decades – New Year's Day 1973 comes immediately to mind – the Gorgie club enjoyed a halcyon sequence of results over a 15-year period from 1983. Prominent in this was Hearts' striker John Robertson, who netted 27 goals against Hibs in this period, never failing to mark a season with at least one goal against the Easter Road outfit. Yet Robertson had once considered an offer to sign for Hibs, only to find the club obdurate in its negotiating style. So Robertson came to Gorgie, scored twice against Hibs in his first derby against them, in 1983, and never looked back. He had to wait no less than seven years for a Scotland cap, while successive national managers from the west of Scotland tried out every other striker they could find, and even used converted defenders, before finally giving in and calling up the Hearts man. Robertson scored within 37 minutes of starting his first game. This was against Romania in 1990, and he followed it up with a second, in the next match, against Switzerland, both games ending in victory. Robbo has retired now, and at the time of writing is serving another club in a 'back room' capacity. Meanwhile, Tynecastle park itself has undergone considerable conversion, although the 1920s grandstand still broods over the ground.

Gorgie residents live within walking distance of the new cinema complex at Fountain Park (see Dalry), although older residents recall that Gorgie had three very characterful cinemas of its own. The Tivoli (or New Tivoli) still stands in Gorgie Road, echoing to the calls of bingo, but it was once famed for its Mickey Mouse club, and it was not unusual for children to queue in their hundreds for entry on a Saturday morning. Cinema historian Brendon Thomas recorded poignantly that when the last individual owner, a Mrs Wood, sold the New Tivoli to a cinema chain in 1961, she left the building in tears. The Lyceum picture house, at the top of Robertson Avenue, seems to have inspired less affection, but Poole's Roxy in Gorgie Road was highly popular until its closure in 1963. Looking now at the façade which remains, it is difficult to imagine the cinema manager being told by a delegation of girl patrons one Saturday morning that they wanted 'less of Shirley Temple' and more 'six-shooting westerns'!

GRANTON

Government: (local) wards 9 (Pilton) and 10 (Granton); (national) Edinburgh North and Leith. Community councils designated for Pilton, Royston/Granton and Drylaw/Telford, but only established in last-named area.

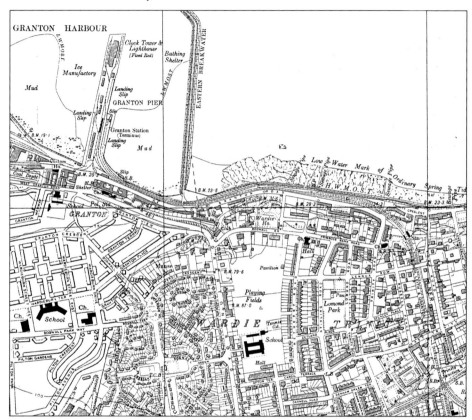

Trams are once again being mooted as the solution to Edinburgh's transport problems, although Scots law concerning local government responsibilities in the event of contractor failure seems to render their reintroduction more difficult than in England, where Sheffield and Manchester have shown the way. Here a vehicle leaves Granton Road station on the 27 service; this was photographed in August 1953, the service being withdrawn two years later. The rail service to and from the station itself ceased in 1962, to leave buses with a monopoly. (W.S. Sellar collection)

Originally part of Cramond parish, Granton began to outstrip its parochial capital by the middle of the 19th century. This was largely because the landowner, the Duke of Buccleuch, saw an opportunity to create a port at Granton unfettered by the commercial restraints with which Edinburgh had bound its port of Leith for centuries. As a result, a 1,700ft-long pier was constructed by engineer James Walker at Granton, handling 130,000 passengers and 410,000 goods tonnage in its first year, 1845. The Duke's presence on the board of the new Caledonian Railway ensured that the port was rail-connected from the west at around that time, with a rival line coming in from Trinity. There was even a station here for the 500ft-long Old Chain Pier (later wrecked in a storm in 1898, but still nominally recalled by an attractive pub).

Granton harbour, although never fitted with a tidal lock, offered ferry facilities to Burntisland for decades. One of the world's first rail ferries, the *Leviathan*, operated here from 1849, although the best-known vessel on the route was probably the *William Muir*, which plied the Forth for no fewer than 60 years from around 1880. After the opening of the Forth rail bridge in 1890, passengers and road vehicles took the place of railway carriages, regular traffic ceasing with World War Two. Later ferry ventures here failed to prosper – surprising perhaps when congestion on the Forth road bridge is considered. Trawlers are no longer a feature of the port here – one of John Grierson's most famous documentaries was *Granton Trawler*, made in 1934 – but nowadays, Granton harbour specialises in heavy plant cargoes, such as power station equipment, while acting as a base for the very active Royal Forth Yacht Club.

Granton Square, shown in around 1955, when trams still contributed to the local transport pattern. In the background can be seen the buildings and paraphernalia of a busy port. Until 1890 rail passengers for Dundee and Aberdeen would pass this way, coming in on the railway on the right of the picture and joining a rail-operated ferry to Burntisland in Fife. This practice ceased with the opening of the Forth Bridge in 1890, but a passenger and freight ferry plied here up until World War Two, with a couple of unsuccessful attempts to revive the route since then. (W.S. Sellar)

The eastern pier of Granton harbour comprises an unusual surface, with stones piled vertically, as can be seen. This was constructed around 1863 as a breakwater for the first pier, built for the Duke of Buccleuch in the 1840s by James Walker. This established Granton not only as a ferry port for Fife traffic, but also as a centre for fishing and for loading specialist cargoes. Nowadays, as the photo shows, it is home to the Royal Forth Yacht Club.

Away from the waterside, Granton once housed the capital's own car factory – owned by, of all people, the City Astronomer, William Peck. His Madelvic vehicles are believed to have succeeded in obtaining a licence to carry mail between Edinburgh and Leith in 1899, but the venture failed to prosper, as did two other vehicle-producing companies occupying the site. Gas supply lasted longer, after processing began here in 1898, having moved from a site next to Waverley Station. The landmark gasometers just west of Granton were of later construction, the most noticeable being the louvred structure erected in 1933. Reaching 275ft in height, this gas-holder had the unusual distinction of being landscaped on the advice of the Royal Fine Arts Commission. Granton was the last producer of natural (i.e. non-North Sea) gas in the UK, production ceasing in 1987.

At the 'business' end of Granton harbour this vessel, the paddle steamer William Muir, *was a perennial feature. For nearly 60 years she plied between here and Burntisland, carrying freight and no fewer than 800,000 passengers after the railway traffic had been diverted across the Forth Bridge from 1890. Only World War Two brought her shuttling to a stop, and the passage has never been successfully reinstated since that time.* (Edinburgh City Libraries)

Not far from Granton is Pilton, a 1930s slum-clearance solution to the prevalent problem at that time of overcrowded housing in central Edinburgh and Leith. West Pilton, between Granton and Ferry Road, was developed first, in 1937, with two and three-room housing being built in terraced and high-rise configurations. The lack of shopping and social facilities should have served as a warning when Muirhouse was planned 15 years later. The reduction in the nearby gas and electronics industries has affected local employment prospects badly, and, with Muirhouse and Craigmillar, this represents the most highly deprived area of the city.

Nowadays Granton, still operating as a port, is shrouded by warehouses along its waterfront, while its hinterland is dominated by housing, from Trinity in the east to Muirhouse in the west.

Gas was produced in central Edinburgh for many years at the New Street works close to Waverley Station, with the producing company being run by the local authority from 1888. As New Street became increasingly cramped the decision was taken to move to a seashore site. So the Granton complex was still new when this picture was taken in 1903, showing the coke yard, complete with screening and loading plants, fronted by the staff. Granton ceased to produce non-North Sea gas in around 1987.
(Edinburgh City Libraries)

HAYMARKET

Government: (local) ward 15 (Murrayfield) and ward 30 (Dalry); (national) Edinburgh Central. Covered by West End community council.

Like Tollcross on the south-west corner of the city centre, Haymarket is a nerve centre where the main roads from Princes Street, and the Old Town, split into westward routes via either Corstorphine or Dalry. A major road redevelopment here in the early 1970s made Morrison Street, Torphichen Street and part of West Maitland Street into one-way thoroughfares, with considerable success in keeping traffic moving. All this meant the moving of the Hearts memorial, but its prominence is undiminished (and its significance is discussed under Gorgie).

Centering on its railway station, opened in 1842 as the eastern terminus of the Edinburgh & Glasgow Railway, Haymarket is a contrasting mix of working-class housing in Dalry, including a 'colony', and a crescent of 'model' houses at Gardener's Crescent. These are in complete contrast to the more measured terraces and crescents of the western New Town to the north.

Haymarket's outstanding landmark is St Mary's Cathedral, located between Manor Place and Palmerston Place. Built over a period of nearly 45 years from 1874, this is Scotland's principal Episcopalian church, and the seat of the Bishop of Edinburgh. Designed by Gilbert Scott, the cathedral's three spires are visible from the Pentlands to the south and from the other side of the firth to the north. The music school next door deservedly enjoys an international reputation.

Probably the most distinguished secular building in the area is Donaldson's School for the Deaf. Opened in 1851, this edifice, visible from the Glasgow Road, was designed by William Playfair and funded from a bequest from James Donaldson. Up to 200 children are educated here, either as day pupils or boarders. They can enjoy the thought that Queen Victoria is rumoured to have offered to exchange Holyrood Palace for Donaldson's, and it represented a choice target for the Zeppelin attack of April 1916. The German crew may have mistaken the school, with its extensive grounds, for a barracks, and unleashed at least one bomb (modest by modern standards) on their way to attack the castle. Fortunately, there was no loss of life here, although a domestic servant suffered a hysterical attack. (For more on this, the only occasion when Scottish civilians were killed by direct enemy action in World War One, see Leith. Although the death-toll on that April night exceeded that incurred on the ground in the Lockerbie disaster of 1988, there is no memorial to the dead of Edinburgh or Leith. Quite the opposite – an inscription in the new Ocean Terminal building in Leith dismisses the losses as 'minor damage').

The palatial appearance of Donaldson's School for the Deaf adds a certain class to the Glasgow Road. This picture was taken not long after completion in 1851, at which time Queen Victoria is believed to have offered to swap it for Holyrood. It came under attack from a German Zeppelin in April 1916, whose crew mistook its lawns for the parade grounds of a military barracks. Fortunately, there were no casualties here, although that was not the case either in Leith or in the Grassmarket. Edinburgh's citizens were quite literally defenceless. (Edinburgh City Libraries)

The Dean Village was once known as the village of the Water of Leith, on which it stands, and where baking and milling were undertaken. Around 1830 the village came to be overshadowed by Telford's great Dean Bridge carrying the Queensferry Road westwards towards the left of this 1860 picture. The photographer was Thomas Begbie, yet another camera artist who followed where Hill and Adamson had led. (Edinburgh City Libraries)

Mention 'Haymarket' to the average citizen and this is the kind of view which comes to mind – of a crossroads constantly being threaded by traffic. This picture shows the way it was in 1952, with a tram picking its way towards Dalry and then on to Stenhouse or Slateford. The crossroads was redesigned in 1972, with West Maitland Street (behind the tram) becoming eastbound only and westbound traffic being diverted through Torphichen Place. All this necessitated the moving of the Hearts' memorial, although this was done sensitively and still occupies a prominent place in the townscape of Haymarket. (Edinburgh City Libraries)

There can be few orphanages as striking as the Dean example of such utilities. Constructed in 1833 to a design by Thomas Hamilton, it is seen here only a couple of decades later in an early Calotype, with part of the Dean Village and Belford Road visible in the foreground. Nowadays, the Dean building is an art gallery, with the work of Leith's Sir Eduardo Paolozzi featuring prominently. This photograph shows the clock which still survives from the old Netherbow Port, dividing Edinburgh from its first suburb, Canongate. (Edinburgh City Libraries)

In the late 1990s, Donaldson's was the subject of press speculation that it might become the home of the proposed Scottish Parliament – speculation which ended abruptly when the headmaster announced that he had not even been consulted about the idea. But Haymarket, with its main roads and railways to west and south-west, was perhaps not a bad suggestion for the Parliament's site.

Just half a mile from the city's West End, and within a few minutes walk from Stockbridge along the river, the Dean Village nestles in the valley of the Water of Leith, with Telford's great bridge brooding above. Completed in 1831, this four-arch structure is 410ft long and towers no less than 100ft above the river bed. The upper parts are hollow, to reduce the weight held up by the piers, and the parapets were raised in 1912 to try to reduce suicides. The nearby Belford Bridge, half a mile to the west, is interesting too, if less dramatic, its single arch crowned with the city's arms.

Curiously, these are the only bridges near the city centre which actually span water – those in central Edinburgh, the North, South, Waverley, Regent, George and King's Bridges – all cross roads or buildings. It was Charles Darwin who, as a student newly arrived in Edinburgh, peered over the North Bridge expecting to see 'a fine river'. The view from the Dean Bridge would have more than sufficed, but was not completed until some six years later.

Originally called the village of the Water of Leith, this self-contained community was famous for meal-milling and bakery products. Now it is a highly attractive residential area, its centrepiece a 19th-century quadrangle called Well Court, accommodating artisans' houses and a hall. New housing has blurred the edges of the old village, but it is still one of Edinburgh's most interesting districts.

KIRKLISTON

*Government: (local) ward 3 (Dalmeny/Kirkliston);
(national) Edinburgh West. Community council.*

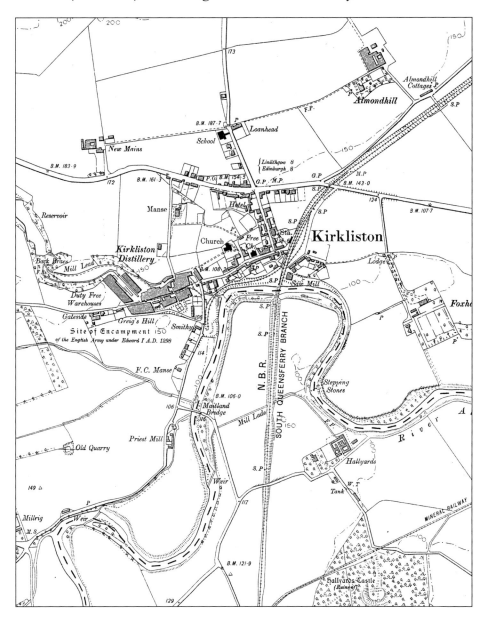

Opposite page: Kirkliston parish church can rival Dalmeny and Duddingston in its claims to antiquity. It dates from the 12th century, and this late Victorian photograph well illustrates its south door, described in the Buildings of Scotland *volume as the church's showpiece. The weathercock atop the belfry is an unusual feature for a Scottish church.* (Edinburgh City Libraries)

To the motorist passing close by on the M9, Kirkliston is a community apparently dominated by one of its major industries, a distillery. It is in fact a pleasant village, formerly in West Lothian, but transferred to Edinburgh District in 1975.

At the time of the *First Statistical Account* in the 1790s, the parish, originally known as Temple Liston, was split 75–25% respectively between what were then known as the counties of Linlithgow and Edinburghshire. At the time, the parish

minister made an appeal for land near villages to be made available to ordinary parishioners on a kind of small-holding or allotment basis 'to give them a property and existence in the country' at a time 'of rapidly increasing cultivation, where a capital is required'. An honourable sentiment, although there is nothing in the *Second Account*, written some 50 years later, to indicate that the minister's plea was granted.

The village has a parish church rivalling Dalmeny and Duddingston's in antiquity, having been dedicated in 1244 and in continuous use ever since. Despite its pleasant surroundings, the village hosts a considerable variety of industry; apart from the distillery, rubber and electronic concerns have made their way to the area from central Edinburgh over the last half century, although the recent trade recession has brought many redundancies. Pink shale bings are evidence of 19th-century mining in the quest for paraffin. Begun by James 'Paraffin' Young in 1850, this was at one time a lucrative extractive industry whose principal drawback was its failure to dispose of its own detritus, still visible today from miles around. The industry centred on Winchburgh, a community dwarfing Kirkliston itself at one time.

The parish of Kirkliston includes Ingliston showground, immediately north of the old A8. Bought by the Royal Highland and Agricultural Society of Scotland in 1958, the site opened as the principal agricultural centre in Scotland two years later.

Local travellers may not associate Edinburgh Airport with Kirkliston, but, in strictly parochial terms, this facility has been realigned from its original site of Turnhouse and penetrates far into Midlothian. Originally built around the village of Turnhouse, this was a World War One airfield hurriedly constructed to provide a base for fighters opposing incoming Zeppelins, Edinburgh being the first – indeed the only – Scottish city to suffer their attentions.

During World War Two, Turnhouse was the spiritual home of 603 City of Edinburgh Squadron, described in a recent volume of military history as the most successful unit to operate in the Battle of Britain (in ratio of sorties to enemy planes destroyed). The squadron features prominently in the classic war history *The Last Enemy*, written by Spitfire pilot Richard Hillary. While the book concentrates on Hillary's own experience, including his fight to recover from burns so severe as to cause his nurses to faint at the sight of him, there is enough about his fellow pilots – 'Uncle' George Denholm, 'Sheep' Gilroy, 'Black' Morton and the doomed MacDonald brothers – to evoke a portrait of a generation where every young man had the potential and opportunity to become a hero. David Ross's biography of Hillary provides a fuller picture of what happened to these Scottish heroes, something Hillary could not have done, as he died in controversial circumstances. He was almost certainly too crippled to have been allowed to fly again, yet he was at the controls when his plane crashed into the Berwickshire countryside in January 1943.

Two years after the end of hostilities, civil operations began to take precedence at Turnhouse, but it was not until 1976 that a new terminal building was constructed, reached by a spur off the M8, and a longer (8,400ft) runway commissioned, running east to west and stretching far from what used to constitute Turnhouse village.

Nowadays, Kirkliston includes Ratho within its area, at least as far as local government is concerned, yet the latter village has its own identity, and constitutes a parish in its own right. 'Perhaps no parish in this country affords more varied and delightful prospects than that of Ratho'. In writing this in 1792, the local parish minister was describing the views from this village some seven miles west of Edinburgh, with as many as 16 Scottish counties visible from the hill above the manse. The view within the parish was considered no less attractive at that time, with a 'salutary' climate giving rise to longevity among Ratho's inhabitants (similar claims were made for Balerno and Currie), and with farming undertaken 'with great spirit and success'.

In the century which followed, a new settlement called Ratho Station grew up to the north of the village, around the station built on the Edinburgh-Glasgow mainline (and closed in the 1960s). The 1975 local government reorganisation 'moved' Ratho and its satellite into Edinburgh, although the existence of the green belt ensures that urbanisation has been kept reasonably in check.

Ratho has a particular attraction for tourists – a wayside pub situated on a basin on the Union Canal. From here, passenger boats wend westwards towards, and over, an impressive aqueduct over the river Almond. Such cruises could be extended in future, when the intended linking of the Union and Forth & Clyde canals is accomplished by means of the new gigantic 'water wheel'. East from Ratho the canal ran into a culvert on the city's western side until recently, so Ratho was, for the last three decades at least, Edinburgh's quayside access to this charming waterway.

Ratho is a former Midlothian village which was absorbed by Edinburgh in 1975. The village is linear, running parallel with, and enlarged by its association with, the Union Canal. Most of the High Street's buildings date from around the time of its construction. (Edinburgh City Libraries)

LEITH

*Origin of name: from the British word 'llaith' meaning a river,
and probably referring to the Water of Leith.
Government: (local) wards 21 (Harbour), 22 (Lorne), 37
(Links) and part of 12 (Newhaven);
(national) Edinburgh North and Leith. Community councils
for Harbour, Bonnington, Links, and Lorne.*

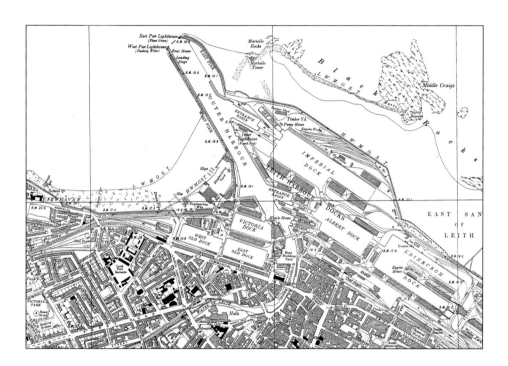

No self-respecting Leither would ever agree that their home town is a suburb of anywhere – especially of Edinburgh! It's no secret that there is a centuries-old rivalry between the capital and its port. At one time that division was a political one, with Leith achieving independence between the years 1833 and 1920. But long before that, there had been a feeling of unease, almost of enmity, between the two communities, and even since reamalgamation there is still something of a coolness. Irvine Welsh has something to say on the subject in his controversial novel *Trainspotting*!

Although the Firth of Forth might be thought of as the dominant stretch of water in the vicinity of Leith, it is in fact the Water of Leith which distinguishes the town, gives it its name and divides North Leith from South. (To the uninitiated, the west bank is the north.) The river rises 22 miles away in the Pentlands, but its joining with the sea has been revolutionised in recent times. In 1969 a new lock installation ensured permanent high tide conditions as far up the river as Great Junction Street.

The river channel was the location for the first mercantile operations in the town, with a quay on the eastern side from early times, later extended seawards in the form of a pier. Known as 'the Shore', it was here that such historical landfalls were made as that of Mary Stewart, Queen of Scots, when she returned from France in 1561 in a haar (advection fog) to claim her kingdom. In 1822 George IV became the first Hanoverian monarch to visit Scotland by landing at the Shore, before going on to Holyrood, where he sported pink tights with his kilt!

Boat-building is believed to have begun here in the early 15th century. By the time of the Union of the Parliaments in 1707, there were eight yards building on the river, with the first dry-dock in the area effective from 1770. The first passenger steamship to cross the Atlantic, the *Sirius*, was built in Leith in 1838, and from 1900 the industry was based almost entirely in the reclaimed area north of the shore-line, hosting such companies as Hawthorns, Ramage & Ferguson, and (ultimately exclusively) Henry Robb. Newcastle-headquartered Hawthorn also built locomotives in Leith at Sherriff Brae, the birthplace of some 425 locos before the 1880s.

Leith's first docks were begun early in the 19th century, and proved so expensive to construct that the city was willing to give Leith its municipal 'independence' rather than pay for them. The East and West Docks – both, confusingly, west of the Water of Leith – were opened in 1806 and 1817 respectively, and were later to earn the additional soubriquet of 'Old Docks'.

This is Leith's lost 'high street', the Kirkgate, pictured in around 1910. Notice the emphasis on entertainment, the Gaiety theatre in the middle-right of the picture, with its tenement front, pediment and ornate lamps, the signs advertising a billiards saloon, and mens' suits for 19s 6d. The theatre, which also showed films from time to time, closed in 1956, and the entire street was swept away not long afterwards. (Edinburgh City Libraries)

These are now filled in, the dock immediately to the north of their site, the Victoria, being opened in 1851, but this is now no more than a frontage for the Scottish Executive building whose car park occupies the site of the two Old Docks.

Further docks were added in 1869 (Albert), 1881 (Edinburgh) and 1904 (Imperial). Coal exports peaked at 2.2 million tons in 1923, but the port has probably survived because it handled a variety of cargoes and was not tied into serving one particular industry. Esparto grass and grain were the principal imports at Leith until around 1950. In the long term, Leith lost cargoes to Glasgow and Grangemouth because of government control measures in two world wars, so by the 1950s was operating with gross over-capacity. A visitor to the docks then would be lucky to see a ship; but North Sea oil changed all that.

As if anticipating the offshore boom, the Leith Dock Commission installed a lock entrance in 1969, maintaining high water in the docks and up the Water of Leith, as previously mentioned. The now-privatised docks (owned by Forth Ports plc) are permanently busy with oilfield support traffic, while grain imports continue. However, ships are no longer built at Leith; the site of the former shipyards facing west across the Western Harbour is now given over to coffee shops and clothing stores (see below). The last vessel to be constructed here was the *St Helen*, a ferry built for the Isle of Wight passage, which was completed in 1984. But Leith-built ships are still to be found around the world. As late as 2001, the French Navy was still using a frigate built at Leith during World War Two – the *Lucifer*, a veteran of the Battle of the North Atlantic – although it is now utilised only for training purposes.

North Leith may have boasted the earliest docks, and today hosts the new Ocean Terminal, but South Leith has had an equally interesting history. The town's famous Roperie was situated just north of the Links and it was from this

Previous page: Leith no longer needs a town hall, having lost its municipal identity in 1920. The building which housed it at the corner of Constitution and Queen Charlotte Streets was designed as the Sheriff Court in 1827, and currently houses Leith Police Station. Not long after opening it was hurriedly converted to a town hall (note the pediment facing southwards), and the former council chamber still exists inside, graced by an Alexander Carse painting of George IV's famous visit of 1822. (Edinburgh City Libraries)

The Pilrig Muddle. This Edwardian photograph shows the problems experienced by travellers between Edinburgh and Leith at the junction of the two municipal tram systems at the corner of Pilrig Street and Leith Walk. Passengers from the port have just alighted from a Leith tram (in the background, with traction pole extended upward) and are joining an Edinburgh cable car to continue citywards. No through journeys were possible after Leith embarrassed its larger rival by introducing electric cars in 1904, until the two systems were amalgamated in 1922. (H. Stevenson collection)

side of the docks that coal was exported directly from the Lothian coalfield. A Martello tower, built to repel possible Napoleonic invasion, was built in 1809 on the 'south' side of the Water of Leith, but is now part of the reclamation project which has produced new filter beds for sewage treatment in the Seafield area.

Sport too has featured prominently on this side of the river. Until the 1830s, Leith was noted for its sands, featuring horse racing for many decades – before being transferred to Musselburgh – while the links hold a special place in the history of golf. It was here, on Leith Links, that golf was given the royal imprimatur in the 15th century and the earliest rules were codified. In 1744 the Honourable Company of Edinburgh Golfers instituted a prize competition to take place on the links, complete with its own set of rules. Golfers at St Andrews failed to follow suit until 10 years later, but within a century, Leith was no longer the leading centre of the game. Writing in the *Edinburgh Encyclopedia*, George McMurdo records that by 1834 the Edinburgh club:

> ... was in a period of eclipse due to the decline of Leith Links owing to overcrowding and related deterioration of the turf... [so] the St Andrews club successfully petitioned King William IV to designate it Royal and Ancient.

The links no longer hosts golf, a sport exiled to Craigentinny from around 1907, but it is still one of the city's best-known parks, complete with the artillery mounds constructed by Oliver Cromwell to bombard royalist forces at Leith Fort.

Leithers have had always had great pride in their community, as recorded by such social historians as James Marshall and George Baird (see bibliography). The 'Foot of the Walk' enjoys the atmosphere of a city centre, although this may not be so obvious since the 1960s demolition of the Kirkgate, with its bustling traffic and highly-popular Gaiety theatre, and its replacement with an anonymous shopping mall.

Leith may have enjoyed official municipal independence for only 87 years (1833–1920), but during that time it established a reputation as a burgh prepared to fight for its existence as a community in its own right. Fifteen Provosts were elected over this period, one of them twice, and the town council constituted 16 members, the councillors taking their seats for the first time on 12 November 1833. As the Leith tolbooth (traditionally the municipal nucleus as well as housing a prison) had been demolished as recently as nine years previously, a town hall had to be hurriedly improvised from the Sheriff Court building. This still stands as the police station at the corner of Queen Charlotte and Constitution Streets, complete with pediment recording the building's service as the municipal centre. Indoors, the council chamber is preserved, presided over by portraits of Leith's provosts, although pride of place goes to an Alexander Carse painting of George IV's landing at Leith in 1822; the actual landfall site is commemorated by a free-standing plaque on the Shore.

Also commemorated with a painting in the council chamber is Ronald Munro-Ferguson, the town's (and at the time the Edinburgh area's) longest-serving MP.

Leith's political history has been touched on in the introduction, but it is not inappropriate to consider this further; in particular, the burgh's earliest parliamentary representatives had to fight to assert the town's independence. This was because the Reform Act which gave birth to Leith as a municipal unit contained a legislative anomaly denying the town income from customs duties – a crucial omission at that time. Despite the fact that Leith's first MP, John Archibald Murray, held a Cabinet post as Lord Advocate, it was not until 1838, five years after its establishment, that the new burgh acquired fund-raising powers.

The town council took its commitments seriously, and in many ways equalled, and sometimes bettered, Edinburgh's administrative record. Leith schools earned an excellent reputation, and their buildings can still be seen, adorned by a magnificent emblem of a schooner under full sail (a good example can be seen at Bonnington Primary). Transport services are dealt with elsewhere in this volume; it suffices to emphasise that Leith enjoyed the benefits of electric tram services some 18 years before Edinburgh got around to introducing them. The town councillors proved too clever for the directors of the Caledonian Railway in the 1890s, forcing the transport concern, about to build an elevated line into the burgh from Ferry Road to Seafield, to agree to peg their fares to less than one penny a mile. This ultimately proved disastrous, making the highly expensive line totally unremunerative for passenger traffic. But what a good example of councillor power! The same group forced the rival North British company to construct a huge terminus called Leith Central at the foot of the Walk, and, while too big for the traffic generated, it at least rendered 49 years service.

Yet more evidence of Leith's relishing of its independence came with the opening of Leith hospital in 1851. For some time it was felt that the growth of the dock area necessitated greater medical facilites nearby for both seaman and dock workers, and the establishment of a charitable hospital fulfilled an important need. Leith hospital enjoyed an excellent reputation, particularly for its out-patient work, being 'nationalised' in 1947 under state control. Unfortunately, its location, in a warren of buildings north of where Great Junction Street crossed the Water of Leith, was not conducive to expansion, nor easy for vehicular access. Leith hospital was reduced to accident and emergency work from 1993 and closed five years later. Its buildings still moulder to this day, their location spurned by the usual housing developments.

Leith itself ceased to exist as a municipal entity in 1920. The increasing cost of public services provided to Leithers – education, fire, transport, street lighting, and so on – could no longer be met from the narrow rateable base in the burgh. And it was almost literally narrow, as Leith failed to push its boundaries east and west to increase the territory on which it could levy rates. Historian James Marshall was particularly critical of the Leith Town Council in his accounts of the amalgamation with Edinburgh. It was perhaps difficult, if not downright unlikely for Leith to have taken over Granton, which was originally part of the parish of

Cramond, and was heavily invested in by business concerns which were opposed to Leith in the 1840s, but Seafield, to the east of Leith, should have been acquired as quickly as possible. In fact this area became part of Edinburgh, but was long under-developed by the city. Much of the site between Leith and Portobello was taken up by a marshalling yard which bus passengers would take more than five minutes to pass, with hardly a train to be seen there during post-war years. Nowadays, Seafield is overwhelmed with warehouses and garish retail developments; would it have been different if Leith had sought legal powers to move its boundaries eastwards?

The pain of merging with Edinburgh was certainly not eased by the actions of the Leith town clerk, who in 1920 conducted a plebiscite (what we nowadays more politely call a referendum) of the town's residents. He found that they opposed amalgamation by a ratio (in approximate thousands) of 29 to 5, or nearly 6 to 1. Unfortunately, his opponents were able to point out that his actions were unauthorised, and there is reason to believe that voters were not given an opportunity to consider both sides of the argument, and particularly the costs of running public services.

The 20th century reintroduced Leithers to the direct experience of war – something they must have thought had been left behind in the days of Cromwell, or at the very latest, those of John Paul Jones, when he attempted to attack Edinburgh with his invading American flotilla in 1779. (The *First Statistical Account* records the recent establishment of nine guns on the west side of Leith Citadel 'occasioned by the appearance of Paul Jones in the neighbourhood'.)

In 1916 Leith shared with Colinton the dubious distinction of being bombed from the air minutes before Edinburgh suffered the same fate. On 2 April of that

Previous page: This atmospheric 1953 shot of milkboys in Leith's Candle Close could have been taken anywhere in the city, but is included as a reminder of how things were done in the 30 or so years after World War Two. Early morning milk deliveries were usually made from a horse-drawn or battery-powered 'float', but smaller dairies sent out boys pushing cast-iron barrows on which two or three crates of milk bottles could be loaded. The barrows were, it appeared, specially designed to cut the shins of the unfortunate trying to push them, and this author still has the scars to prove it. And all for 12s a week! (Edinburgh City Libraries)

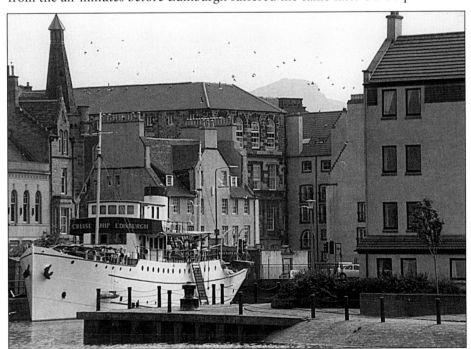

A telephoto shot of Leith Shore from the west bank of the river. The Cruise Ship, *a floating restaurant and function suite, is prominent, and behind it are the buildings of the Shore, the earliest part of Leith to be built up as a maritime complex. The top of Arthur's Seat can just be seen surmounting the view.*

Leith has its own Assembly Rooms, an impressive building located in Constitution Street. The centre of the frontage consists of a pediment supported by massive Ionic pillars. Completed in 1810, before Leith became a burgh, the rooms were used for social functions until about two decades ago, but are now given over to commercial use. (W. Findlay)

year one of two Zeppelin dirigibles flew over Leith, and its crew dropped bombs by hand. The commanders of *L14* and *L22* had planned to attack naval vessels at Rosyth, but the ferocity of the anti-aircraft fire there forced them to turn aside to seek targets in the Scottish capital, and its port of Leith.

Shamefully, not a single gun was available to fire at them; indeed, as related under Colinton, attacked by *L22*, the local authorities had not even troubled to adopt the English system of signalling a warning by lowering and raising gas pressure piped for domestic lighting. So lacking was civil defence advice that the largest death-toll in the city centre occurred in the Grassmarket, where 11 people perished after actually coming out of their houses to view the monster aircraft above. This does not appear to have caused the toll in Leith. Although there is evidence that the German crew of *L14* attempted to hit warehouses, the inevitable 'collateral damage' resulted in two Leithers being killed, one of them a baby, in or near Commercial Street. Curiously, an inscription in the new Ocean Terminal building records that the raid caused only 'minor damage'.

Ironically, or perhaps appropriately, it is in Leith that one of the most curious of war memorials can be found, and its curiosity value stems partly from its vintage. Situated above a warehouse in Pitt Street can be seen a low-relief with an inscription commemorating 'German valour' by showing enemy soldiers killing innocent civilians. It is dated 1914, a record of what the community of the time

Leith has been 'discovered' in recent years as centre for marine tourism, hosting the Tall Ships Race in 1995, and the International Festival of the Sea will be held there in 2003. This 1995 shot shows the Albert Dock complete with tall ships visiting, while on the left can be seen an 1890s hydraulic crane, complete with operating cabin. The Ocean Terminal, better known to tourists and city dwellers alike, is west of here.

felt was an accurate portrayal of the new enemy. While hardly acceptable nowadays, with German people rightfully regarded as key partners in a European community becoming ever more closely integrated, the memorial at Pitt Street is an almost unique physical record of how British people viewed Germany –

Leith's Ocean Terminal opened in October 2001. It is a retail mall facing the Western Harbour, complete with multiplex cinema, department stores and the biggest coffee shop you are likely to find anywhere. Moored outside is the former royal yacht Britannia, *a Mecca for visitors from all over the UK and beyond. The complex has everything except an ocean!* (Beattie Media)

after all, how many other war memorials have a *sarcastic* inscription? Nor can there be many commemorating a war *before* civilian casualties were suffered in that particular town, the first Scots civilians being killed by direct enemy action two years later in this war to end all wars.

1915 was a particularly horrendous year for Leith, with the loss of more than 200 soldiers in a single incident. No French or Flanders battlefield claimed them; their lives were lost in Britain's worst-ever rail crash at Quintinshill, near Gretna Green. After training at Larbert, the men of a Leith-raised battalion of the Royal Scots were travelling on the first stage of a posting to Gallipoli when their train, composed of wooden gas-lit coaches, antiquated even by the standards of the day, collided with two other trains in a conflagration in which 227 perished. The railway signalmen involved were arrested and tried for manslaughter, and it is immensely to the credit of Leithers that there was no demonstration against the two wretched individuals when they were tried at Edinburgh's High Court. The soldiers who lost their lives were buried in a mass grave in Rosebank Cemetery, the site visible from Broughton Road, marked by a red sandstone cross of Celtic design. Unfortunately, the commemorative plaque at the cemetery gates gives the wrong year for the interment.

World War Two opened with much aerial activity in the Forth area, and a large proportion of the city's 20 bombing casualties were killed in Leith or north Edinburgh. A bomb landing near the junction of Commercial Street and Great Junction Street blew a complete section of tram points clear out of the road surface. Just to add to local people's problems, artillery men stationed on Inchkeith in February 1940 fired a six-inch shell over the bows of a trawler about to stray into a minefield. The trawler obeyed the warning, but the shell skipped along the surface of the Forth and bounced into Leith! Mercifully, nobody was killed when it ended its journey in a house in Salamander Street. The same could not be said of the bomb attack in Leith's George Street in the summer of the same year, when six people were killed.

As the violent 20th century drew to its close, Leith was seriously mooted as the site for the Scottish Parliament. This of course is now sited at Holyrood, but the port, with no shortage of available land, was one of the locations considered for a new building. Interestingly, it was Leith's poor terrestrial transport links which appear to have removed it from the equation – there is no dual carriageway into

Leith from south, east or west, no modern tramway and no railway station. It was a cruel irony for a community which, when an independent burgh, operated electric trams nearly 20 years ahead of its city neighbour, and boasted no fewer than four railway termini, one of them – Leith Central – among Scotland's 10 largest. No other British community has lost four rail termini, to be left with none.

Leith nearly had its own airport, the Dock Commission seeking to offer a suitable stretch of water in the Western Harbour for flying boat operations in the early 1930s. Despite slow and often discourteous correspondence from the Air Ministry, LDC were still applying for a flying boat licence as late as 1959, when it was pointed out to the commissioners that no such planes still operated commercially. This particular stretch of water now laps against the new Ocean Terminal, opened in October 2001, combining an extensive retail development with a 12-screen cinema and port facilities for cruise liners. The former royal yacht *Britannia* is moored nearby. Purchased by Forth Ports in 1998, this is of course a Scottish-built vessel, and some unnecessary antipathy appeared in the Glasgow media at the sight of 'their' ship ending its days on the opposite side of Scotland. Yet Glasgow's bid to preserve *Britannia* would have been dependent on a hefty investment from central Government – which was, after all, attempting to clear the vessel off the defence budget, not start financing an urban recovery scheme in the Govan area. In reality, the only community which might feel it had a moral claim to this interesting, if not outstandingly historical, vessel, is Clydebank, where it was built.

Racing and golf may have deserted Leith now, but at least football is still associated with the port. Despite this association, to treat the history of Hibernian FC as part of Leith's story is perhaps a little misleading. Although the media frequently refer to Hibs as a Leith club – and a recent history based on players' interviews was called *Sunshine on Leith* – the club was actually formed in the Canongate district of Edinburgh in 1875. Craigentinny was once their home ground, and the present base at Easter Road has been occupied by the club since the 1930s. It is situated between that thoroughfare and Hawkhill, while the banked terracing, now replaced by modern seating accommodation opposite the new stand, used to loom over Lochend Pond, described under Restalrig.

The club's history can only be summarised here. Formed originally from YMCA members, Hibs became professional when the 20th century dawned, winning the Scottish Cup in 1902 (an achievement the club has yet to repeat), and the First Division championship in the following year. Far and away the finest period in the club's history was the eight or so years following World War Two, when, with the 'Famous Five' forward-line mesmerising defences everywhere, three league trophies were captured in five years, with a fourth title being lost only on goal average. Smith, Johnstone, Reilly, Turnbull and Ormond were the names on everybody's lips, their line broken only by the transfer of Bobby Johnstone to Manchester City in 1955.

A number 25 tram negotiates the single-track section in Leith's Duke Street on its way to Craigentinny, seven years before its withdrawal in 1954. The site to the left nowadays comprises Leith Waterworld (closed at the time of writing) and a Co-op store, but the picture allows a glimpse of the roof of Leith Central station, the biggest built in Britain in the 20th century. It was the product of a deal between the North British railway company and the Edinburgh and Leith town councils to allow additional tracks through Princes Street Gardens, the 'pay off' being that the company had to build a Leith terminus they believed unnecessary. So badly publicised was it on opening day that the local minister failed to find its entrance and stumbled into a notorious pub by mistake! (Edinburgh City Libraries)

The Greens took their skills into Europe that year, becoming the first British club to compete in the European Cup, thanks to imaginative investment in floodlighting. The club did well in their only appearance in the competition, reaching the semi-final, although their finest achievement in Europe was to knock Barcelona out of the Fairs Cup (now the UEFA Cup) in 1961. This was no isolated incident – Hibs defeated Real Madrid in a 1964 friendly (Puskas and all), and knocked five goals past Dino Zoff playing in goal for Italian league-leaders Napoli in 1967.

Under Gorgie, where the history of Heart of Midlothian is briefly featured, the city's traditional 'derby' between the two sides is looked at from a maroon viewpoint. It is only right and proper to examine it from the other side too! Undoubtedly, the most sensational derby match in the last 50 years took place at Tynecastle on New Year's Day 1973. Hearts went into the match with a good side, but Hibs were 'Turnbull's Tornadoes', a charismatic 11 coruscating with the skill of such stars as John Brownlie and Alex Cropley, and captained by Pat Stanton. Although Hearts started brightly, Hibs were able to use a training-ground routine for their first corner – one previously effective only against Besa of Albania – and Jimmy O'Rourke put the Greens one up. Goals by Alan Gordon, Arthur Duncan, Alex Cropley, and Duncan again, meant that Hibs were five up before half-time! Two more goals by O'Rourke and Gordon completed an astonishing result in a game where the Hearts central defenders seemed to be meeting one another for the first time.

Hibs promptly went to the top of the table on that day, much to the astonishment of the Glasgow press and the annoyance of the sporting gods. In the very next game, Brownlie tragically broke a leg, and the Hibs' XI were found to be exactly that – 11. There was no depth to the squad, and the season ended in failure, despite sterling contributions from newcomers Des Bremner and Tony Higgins.

At the present time, Hibernian have concentrated their resources on a complete rebuilding of their ground, something of an achievement, considering that an ill-advised share issue lost the club control over the ownership of its own ground for a time in the 1990s. With this own goal rubbed from the record book, Hibernian faces the future with some confidence, particularly with the high standard of management it has enjoyed in the last three years. Even so, the team continues to enthuse and exasperate in almost equal measure.

Further reading:

Marshall, J.S. *The life and times of Leith* John Donald. 1986.

   Old Leith at leisure Edina, 1976.

Mowat, S. *The Port of Leith: its history and its people* Forth Ports/John Donald.

LIBERTON

*Government: (local) ward 53 (Alnwickhill);
(national) Edinburgh South. Community council.*

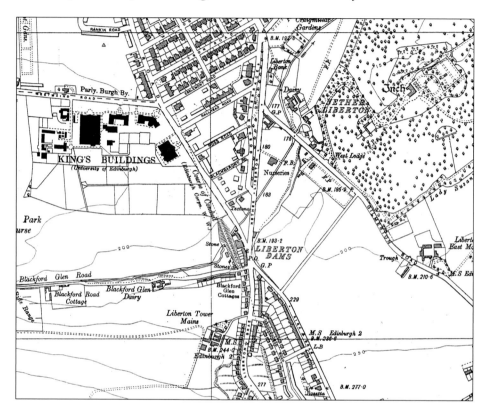

Historians now dispute whether this placename does in fact denote a 'lepers' town' outside the city, there being records of a community at Liberton some 140 years before the disease was recognised in the capital.

Writing in the *First Statistical Account*, in 1786, the local minister claimed that Liberton was the second most populous parish in Edinburgh, with 3,500 souls, although about a fifth of that total lived in Gilmerton. There were no fewer than 20 seams of coal exposed at that time, and there was also a limeworks. The minister was most concerned about the behavioural standards of his parish, recording that people's morals 'are not so unexceptional as could be wished; and no wonder, when they live in the neighbourhood of such a city as Edinburgh'. His meaning is not crystal-clear, but doesn't sound too complimentary!

Modern day Liberton straddles the top of its brae on the A701 south of the city centre, and is predominately residential. The university's King's Buildings campus is situated at the foot of the brae, and the Savacentre shopping complex is a new development. The area includes the Roman Catholic cemetery at Mount Vernon, Liberton Hospital, and an excellent High School.

The last-named is heir to a considerable educational legacy; at one time

Liberton Tower from the north, during a rare heavy snowfall. Built around 1605, the tower has recently been modernised and made available as a residence. It overlooks the valley of the Braid Burn, described by an official geological publication as being almost 'lost' in such a wide valley.

Liberton had its own school board, administering schools at Burdiehouse, Gilmerton, Niddrie and Craigmillar. The minister writing the *Second Statistical Account*, in 1839, recorded that there were 10 schools in the parish, although only one was supported from parish funds, and he personally knew of some 70 children who went uneducated. Clearly Scotland's reputation for free education for all is not entirely deserved. The board came under the jurisdiction of Midlothian County Council in 1919, but was transferred to the Edinburgh authority two years later.

The most historic building in the area is Liberton Tower, brooding over the city from the eastern extremity of the Braid Hills. Four storeys in height, this structure dates back to the early 1500s, built by the Dalmahoy family and purchased by Edinburgh's provost William Little in 1587. A feature of the tower was the retractable wooden staircase, which, with the main entrance being on the first floor, was a useful deterrent to unwanted visitors. Unfortunately, the tower's spartan nature also deterred residents, and the family soon moved to nearby Liberton House, itself a building with a traditionally Scottish appearance. Both tower and house have been attractively restored in recent years.

Just south of Liberton, opposite the opening to Mortonhall Crematorium, is the site of the Balm Well. Associated with St Katherine, the well's waters contain minerals in suspension believed to benefit those with skin problems. This claim was sufficient to warrant the protection of James VI before he moved south to London in 1603, but the royal connection attracted the unwelcome attentions of Cromwell's followers in the mid-17th century, when its site was damaged. The subsequent Restoration saw the well rebuilt, and it is now commemorated within a new housing development.

At Cameron Toll retail centre, the Braid Burn has been culverted, and is now treated with considerable respect by the occupiers of the site! Officially regarded as Edinburgh's second river (second to the Water of Leith), it is classified by Scottish Natural Heritage as a Class A river, with a rich biodiversity of fauna and flora. Rising in the Pentlands near Colinton, it meets the sea (as the Figgate) at Portobello.

The retail industry came to the Liberton area in a big way in the early 1980s, when land close to the Inch was developed as the Cameron Toll shopping centre. Covering 22,000sq ft, the site includes Sainsbury's and BHS. However, the developers soon discovered why the land had been undeveloped for so long – it was a flood plain for the Braid Burn. The manager of one of the smaller shop units still recalls being asked to come to the shop urgently, when the water level topped the four foot mark! The Braid Burn is now shackled with miniature Thames-type barriers, but no one should doubt its potential power – it claimed a life in the Hermitage of Braid in 1998.

Also, just 'down the hill' from Liberton are the King's Buildings. This 86-acre site is the science campus of Edinburgh University, its construction first begun in 1920. Also based here are the Scottish Agricultural College's Edinburgh building, and the northern headquarters of the British Geological Survey. With the Royal Observatory just up on Blackford Hill nearby (see Newington), and the new Royal Infirmary to the east, the scientific centre of the city seems to have moved to the southern suburbs.

MARCHMONT

Origin of name: named for Hume Campbell estate in Berwickshire.
Government: (local) wards 47 (Marchmont) and 48 (Sciennes); (national) Edinburgh South. Marchmont and Sciennes community council.

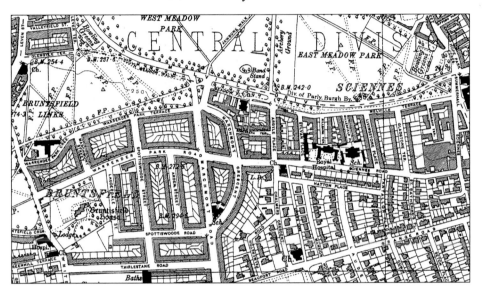

An area almost wholly covered by tenements, Marchmont lies to the south of the Meadows, providing a useful dormitory for those who work at the Royal Infirmary or study at the university. It has its own community council, but otherwise fails to give the impression of a self-contained community, with too few shops and even fewer places of employment or entertainment.

The area features prominently as the dormitory area for numerous characters in the medical novels of Colin Douglas (Colin Currie), most of them employed at the 'Institute' on the opposite side of the Meadows. In one of the earlier novels, the narrator Dr Campbell comments on the waste of time in having to attend committee meetings to discuss a new infirmary building. He would be surprised now, as indeed are many 'real' citizens, to discover that one is soon to be opened far from the Lauriston location, in a new building springing up at Little France (see Gilmerton). Another fictional 'resident' is Inspector John Rebus, the hard-bitten detective created by Ian Rankin. His 'address' is in Arden Street, running parallel to Marchmont Road. Perhaps one day there will a plaque here, so popular has Rebus become.

Marchmont forms the southern boundary of the Meadows, but is itself built on part of what was once the Burgh Muir. Just to emphasise the former extent of this meadow, and not forgetting the Burgh Loch which was drained to produce much of it, a glance at two place-names nearly two miles apart is informative.

Bruntsfield post office is actually called 'Burghmuirhead' – an even more specific indication than the nearby Boroughmuir School – while off Buccleuch Street, over to the east, a lane carries the name 'Boroughlochlane'. The spelling may be different but the geographical feature was the same. Sir Walter Scott recorded the mustering of the Scottish army on the Muir through the words of his fictional character Marmion who:

> from the crown of Blackford,
> saw that martial scene upon the bent so brown,
> a thousand pavilions, white as snow,
> spread all the Borough-moor below,
> upland and dale and down;
> a thousand did I say?
> I ween, thousands upon thousands there were seen,
> that chequered all the heath between the streamlet and the town.

The 'streamlet' was the Jordan Burn, south of, and not part of, Marchmont. But Scott's description of this 1513 scene hints at the full extent of the Meadows, formally declared a public park – and one reduced to 58 acres in Victorian times. The army described was preparing to march on England, but kept a disastrous appointment with the English reserve army at Flodden Field, with James IV dying among the carnage.

The Meadows themselves are perhaps lucky to survive as they have. In 1873 a carriage road was proposed to run north and south through Middle Meadow Walk, and, if implemented, would have resulted in the park being bisected by what would inevitably have become a trafficked connection between Marchmont Road on the south side and Forrest Road on the north. Landscape gardener Edward Kemp successfully campaigned against this potentially damaging development, arguing it would save Newington residents a mere 60 seconds in every trip into town. (Look how Links Place has completely destroyed the

viability of Leith Links as a golf course for Edinburgh's once-independent port).

In the 20th century, there were proposals to build a freight-only railway tunnel east-west across the Meadows in 1949, and then a six-lane elevated motorway in the sixties. We can thank the Cockburn Association for opposing this desecration, which seems almost unbelievable nowadays, but which emphasises that conservationists must be ever-vigilant in protecting the city's assests – of which the Meadows is undoubtedly one.

The eastern end of Marchmont is known as Sciennes, believed to be named after St Catherine of Siena, and this is home to the Royal Hospital for Sick Children. In its 1894 building, moved from a smaller site at Lauriston, this is an internationally renowned centre for paediatric care, and it is shaming to see hospitals such as this having to appeal for public support in the form of voluntary contributions.

Until 1985 Sciennes had a single factory, Bertram's, producing paper-making equipment. It was sited almost opposite the Royal Dick Veterinary College at Summerhall. The 'Dick Vet' was Scotland's first college of its kind, and continues to be its most important. Begun by William Dick in 1833, it was not until Edinburgh University became actively involved in the college's administration that it was able to firmly establish itself over other veterinary colleges in the city, so necessary was this branch of science at a time when all road transport was still literally horse-powered. The Summerhall building dates from 1916, its equine

Marchmont Road looking south in around 1910. With its tenement canyons, this is one of the few areas of Edinburgh, or indeed any city, which can be recognised almost instantly. The only features to have vanished in the last century are the tramlines, which included a conduit running between the rails to provide traction in the form of an endless rope powered from the nearest tram depot, the gas lighting, and the tree foliage to the left of the picture. The principal addition to the local scene nowadays is of course traffic. (Edinburgh City Libraries)

Top: A serried rank of tenements 'look' eastward along Strathearn and Beaufort Roads to the Grange. One of the major problems Marchmont has nowadays is that the area's residents are unable to park outside – or sometimes anywhere near – their front door. This is however an inevitable consequence of tenement life, a legacy of a time when it was inconceivable that every household would have its own mode of transport, let alone more than one. The two horseless-carriage family was not dreamed of when these buildings were feued!

Bottom: Marchmont is separated from the city centre by the Meadows. This is what remains of the Burgh Muir and loch, an important 'lung' for city dwellers, particularly those in Marchmont, almost all of whom have no garden. Eternal vigilance is required by citizens to ensure that the Meadows are not erased out of existence. Melville Drive running east and west through the area introduces high-speed traffic into the location, and in the last 50 years the authorities have threatened to run both an underground railway (for freight only!) and a six-lane highway through the Meadows.

statue round the corner in Summerhall Square unusual in not requiring a Haig or a Wellington to complete it!

Nowadays Marchmont can claim to be almost entirely a dormitory for the city across the sward, but it is an interesting suburb nevertheless.

MERCHISTON

*Origin of name: early British for 'the farm
belonging to Merchiaun'.
Government: (local) ward 45;
(national) Edinburgh Central and South.Community council.*

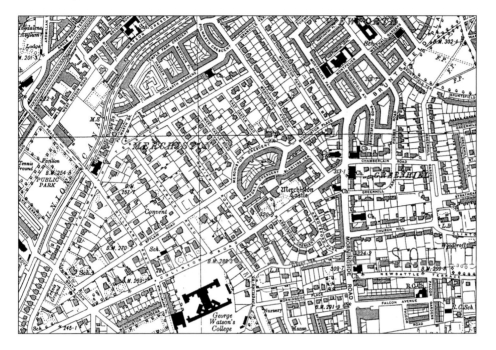

Churchhill, seen here on 11 August 1953, is usually regarded as part of Morningside, although the local authority decided that the 'frontier' between Merchiston and Morningside would be Newbattle Terrace, best-known as the venue for the Dominion cinema. This shot shows a service 14 tram turning northwards to head for Granton; it will return to Churchhill via Marchmont. (R.J.S. Wiseman)

An indeterminate area south of Gorgie and Dalry and north of Morningside, Merchiston's housing represents a complete cross-section of the city's, ranging from tenement to villa, with two 'colonies' of artisans' houses. One of these is situated next to the former Merchiston railway station, closed in 1965, and there is no recognisable main road or high street for this community to configure around. There is, however, an active community council.

The principal fortified building in the area is Merchiston Tower. Dating from the 15th century, the tower is famed as the home of the well-known Napier family, and not surprisingly has been incorporated into the campus of Edinburgh's third university, named for John Napier. Inventor of logarithms, and designer of an armoured vehicle, John Napier was one of Scotland's most innovative sons. His works included a mechanical computing device, known as 'Napier's Bones', and, although hardly a forerunner of today's computers, his achievement prompts the thought that Edinburgh is perhaps losing the opportunity of establishing a Museum of

The Union Canal runs through Merchiston, and can offer an attractive, if perilous, walk for local people. (The peril comes from thoughtless cyclists who treat the towpath as a racetrack). This picture shows the waterway, opened in 1822, overhung by willows near Harrison Park, with the Edinburgh Canal Society's boathouse just out of sight to the right. A floating restaurant can be seen in the left background.

Computing. Where better to create one than in the Scottish capital, the birthplace of one of history's most illustrious inventor/scientists?

In November 2001, Merchiston lost perhaps its most illustrious author, with the death of Dorothy Dunnett. A resident of Colinton Road, not far from Napier's tower, Dorothy had used her masterly knowledge of Scottish history to produce a series of chronicle novels, which, though fictional, were so imbued with authenticity as to engender a worldwide following.

Previous page: Perhaps the most instantly recognisable building in the district of that name is Merchiston tower, the one-time home of the Napier family. This 1957 view shows its condition before it was imaginatively incorporated into the 1960s campus of Napier University. The most famous of the Napiers was John, whose achievements in devising logarithms, a primitive computer and designs for martial vehicles, virtually qualify him as the Scottish Michaelangelo. An excuse for Edinburgh to establish a computer museum, surely? (Edinburgh City Libraries)

M O R N I N G S I D E

Name: topographical in origin, believed to indicate land looking south from Churchhill.
Government: (local) North Morningside, South Morningside; (national) Edinburgh South and Edinburgh Pentlands, duplicated by MSPs. Morningside community council.

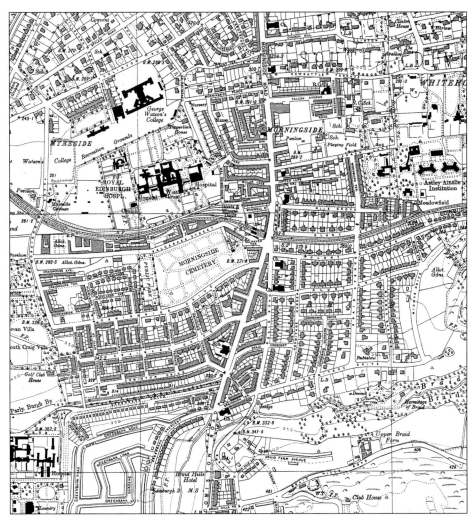

First identified on maps in the mid 18th-century, Morningside developed from a village community straddling the major road to the south-west. It received a boost with the arrival of the Edinburgh Suburban and Southside Railway (the 'Sub') in 1884, whose passenger station at Morningside's famous Clock Junction proved convenient for commuting and whose freight sidings in Maxwell Street allowed the transfer of consumer goods for the developing south side of the city.

From the final years of the 19th century a villa community grew up in Morningside, the well-to-do residents able to enjoy the hybrid nature of the

location – with the city easily accessible by train and cable-car to the north, and the Hermitage of Braid and Braid Hills within strolling distance to the east and south.

No fewer than four hospitals were established in the area. The Royal Edinburgh (the principal psychiatric hospital in the east of Scotland) opened here in 1813, the City Hospital was created as a fever hospital at Greenbank in 1903, only to close five years short of its centenary, and the Astley Ainslie, a convalescent facility, was created in the 1920s within the grounds of a number of villa properties to the east of the suburb. To the west was Craighouse, a satellite of the Royal Edinburgh, now a campus of Napier University, Edinburgh's third seat of learning.

To service these, and shops which sprang up along the main road, tenement accommodation proliferated at the end of the 19th century on and around Morningside Road and Comiston Road, which comprised the main-thoroughfare, nowadays known as the A702. With Edinburgh having no motorway connection with London – the largest British city to be so deprived – this road provides the shortest route to connect with the M6, the gateway to the south. Not surprisingly, this results in chronic traffic congestion on the main street of the suburb; curiously, it appears to be at its worst at lunch-times. Morningside decides to have its rush-hour at a different time to everyone else!

Morningside is distinguished in hosting one of Scotland's few remaining

The number 16 tram service had less than a week to survive before closure when this picture was taken on 6 September 1956. Vehicle No.180 looks much the worse for wear as it prepares to head for the Braids terminus, before running down again to Granton. A spur leads off to the left for the Morningside terminus in Belhaven Terrace, which lasted for another three months, until the end of tram services in the capital. Nowadays, this is a very busy junction on the A702, a road forced to carry much Edinburgh-London traffic. (W.S. Sellar collection)

Braidburn Valley park is one of Britain's most beautiful urban open spaces. This southward-looking view shows the Pentland ridge in the background, with the Braid Burn flowing out of the left of the picture, under the A702, and into the Hermitage of Braid. Braidburn Valley includes an open-air theatre, shamefully underused, its grass seating separated from the stage and orchestra pit (more of a trio or quartet pit!) by the flowing waters of the burn.

Morningside tenements in Maytime. This shot was taken in Woodburn Terrace, showing the Edinburgh tenement at its most solid and respectable. Tenements or 'lands' first sprang up in Edinburgh's Old Town, where space was at a premium within the city walls. It was continued into the suburbs for purely commercial reasons – a three-storey 'stair' like one of those illustrated can incorporate up to 12 separate households.

suburban cinemas. The Dominion has been in the hands of the Cameron family since it opened in 1938, and now boasts four auditoria and a menu of first-run films enjoyed by a large clientele. There is a pleasant bar down a staircase decorated with photographs of the many Hollywood stars who have found their way to the 'Dommy' over the years, to be greeted by the kilted Camerons.

A macabre footnote to Morningside's history lies in its claim to be the last place in Scotland where convicted criminals were executed at the site of their crime. On 25 January 1815 two Irishmen were hanged at the corner of Braid

Road and Comiston Terrace; their punishment for a highway robbery committed on that very spot. A commemorative plaque is set into the road at the location.

Despite the good cheer of its citizens – whose patience and understanding towards psychiatric patients has been frequently commented upon by health professionals – Morningside has somehow been saddled with an unenviable reputation for prudishness, snobbery, and sexual hypocrisy. When BBC 2 produced a programme on this in 1994, it failed to find local residents who fitted the expected profile, and disgracefully employed actors to portray Morningsiders with the required degree of snobbishness and hypocrisy!

The 'terminal terminus' might be the description of this photograph of trams waiting in Belhaven Terrace, just off Morningside Road, before operating the number 23 service down to Granton. This was the last service in Edinburgh to be operated by tram, in November 1956, and the corner here is now almost unrecognisable. Over to the right a bank building occupies the corner, and drivers coming down Comiston Road would take a dim view of tram 66 jutting out into the A702! (W.S. Sellar collection)

MURRAYFIELD

Origin of name: named from estate owned by Murray family.
Government: (local) ward 15;
(national) Edinburgh Central. Community council.

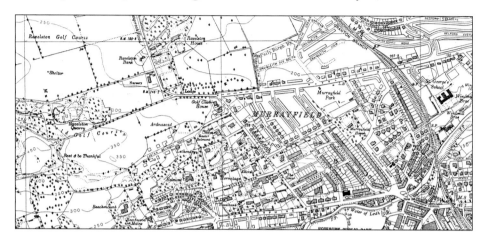

A residential area, Murrayfield has grown westwards from the hamlet of Coltbridge (Roseburn), the area north of the Glasgow Road being feued for housing in the mid-19th century as far as the present day zoo. The earliest existing dwelling in the vicinity is the 16th-century Roseburn House, which no longer surveys meadows north to the Water of Leith – although a modern park is nowadays better than yet another built-up area – and the house is now dwarfed by the 67,500-seat Murrayfield Stadium, the finest sports venue in Scotland.

Rugby Union has been played here since 1925, when the Scottish Rugby Union dropped 'football' from its title and moved here from Inverleith, where international matches were previously played. Undersoil heating was installed as early as 1959, and, following chaotic conditions when an estimated 104,000 turned up to see Scotland v Wales in 1975, an all-seater stadium was created. Edinburgh's – and (marginally) Scotland's – largest sporting complex, Murrayfield is also hired out for pop concerts, and for a while entertained American-style football.

Murrayfield's second sport is based just north-west of here – at the ice-rink. Completed in 1939, it was immediately requisitioned by the defence authorities as World War Two dawned, and the new facility did not take on its intended function until 1952. With a 60 x 33m icepad, Murrayfield rink is one of the biggest in the country, with a thriving ice-skating club and the headquarters of the Scottish Ice Skating Association. Ice hockey is still popular here, although the team has been unable to retain its premier status and the rink's seating and changing rooms could do with some upgrading.

Municipal boundaries include Ravelston in Murrayfield, which means that this district description must include two national art galleries. In 1984 the Scottish

The A8, looking from Murrayfield towards Haymarket. In the foreground is the metalwork of the former Caledonian railway bridge on the branch line from Princes Street to Leith North and Granton. This has been imaginatively preserved as part of a walk and cycle-way, but might have been better remaining as part of a suburban light railway system to lift some of the burden from the city's buses. There are few other British cities as dependent on one mode of public transport as Edinburgh.

Gallery of Modern Art moved to Belford Road from Inverleith House (in the Royal Botanic Garden). Housed in the former John Watson's school, the gallery has benefited in recent years from the Penrose and Keiller bequests, two of Europe's most important collections of surrealist art. There is a small sculpture park, and at the time of writing the grounds are being landscaped by Charles Jencks. Opposite the SGMA is the Dean Gallery, a former education centre devoted mainly, if not exclusively, to the work of Edinburgh's own Sir Edward Paolozzi. Unlike the older gallery across the street; indeed, unlike the main National Gallery on the Mound, art in the Dean Gallery has to be paid for, to be seen.

South of the Water of Leith, brewing and railways gave Murrayfield an industrialised appearance in decades gone by, but new housing developments are now reinforcing Murrayfield's residential image.

A view of Roseburn looking west into Murrayfield. Rugby fans on their way to the ground from the city centre will take the opening to the left, into Roseburn Street. Just round the corner on the main road is the bridge which carries the A8 across the Water of Leith. To the right of the picture is the former site of Murrayfield railway station, ideally placed for local commuters, but closed since 1962.

NEWCRAIGHALL

Origin of name: new settlement from Scots 'Craig Haugh', from land nearer the Esk.
Government: (local) wards 57 (Craigmillar) and 58 (Duddingston); (national) Edinburgh East and Musselburgh. Craigmillar community council.

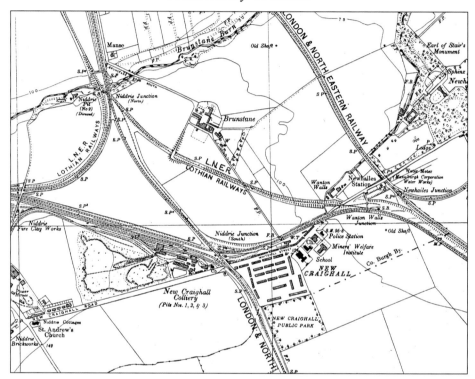

Newcraighall village looking west. This picture dates from the autumn of 2001; had it been taken 30 years earlier the view from this angle would have been filled by the buildings of the local coal mine, dominated by its winding gear tower. This mine thrived on its 'Klondyke' seam, a vein of mineral which stretched out under the Forth. Much of the village housing has been modernised, although some of the original cottages along the main road survive.

Another shot of Newcraighall cottages. With its through road sensibly traffic-calmed, the area probably receives less traffic going to and from the retail development some half-mile to the west than might otherwise be the case. At one time literally surrounded by railways, the area now has the new A1 road system overflying it.

Newcraighall, on Edinburgh's north-eastern frontier, is a former mining village, similar to hundreds once common in coalfields all over Britain. Nowadays its rows of single-storey terraces have been replaced by more modern housing, although there are still terraced cottages on the main road. No longer overlooked by the winding tower of the nearby colliery, Newcraighall has lost much of its mining atmosphere.

Coal had been dug here for centuries, the Inveresk parish minister noting in 1839 that the largest steam-engine in Scotland was employed to pump out the mines at Newcraighall. It generated 140hp and cost the then-astronomical sum of £6,000. But it was the opening of the Klondyke seam in 1897, a year after a gold rush in Canada (which gave the new face its name) that saw the village reach its peak as a mining centre. By the 1920s, 1,000 men were producing a quarter of a million tons of coal a year, some of the underground galleries reaching out under the Forth.

Geological problems forced the pit's closure in 1968, and the nearby Kinnaird retail park nowadays offers less dangerous employment for local people. One of the city's biggest fire stations is situated here, a sensible positioning considering the construction of the new A1 at this point, running at right-angles to the village street. This is distinguished by a modernistic sculpture 'To the Spirit of Community', created by Jake Harvey in 1989.

The Scottish Film Council has commemorated Bill Douglas with a plaque in Newcraighall. There can be few mining villages anywhere that have produced a talented film director – Yorkshire's Tony Richardson is one possible rival – and his short working life means that he may not have been able to give us his best filmic efforts.

Although regarded as a mining community, Newcraighall had its usual share of services supporting local agricultural and transport ventures, and the blacksmith was one of them. This 1928 shot shows a couple of local laddies helping out down at the smiddy's in a manner that would give a health and safety official a few nightmares! (Edinburgh City Libraries)

The Newcraighall community has made its impact on the silver screen, the 1972 film *My Childhood* launching the tragically all too brief career of local film director Bill Douglas (1934–1991). There can be few members of the film community who have forged an international reputation on such a limited number of films – four in fact, three of them chronicling Douglas's own life growing up in Newcraighall, emerging into the wider world, and serving in the army. While not totally original – his autobiographical style owed much to François Truffaut – it was nevertheless an astonishing filmic achievement for a creative young man from a depressed environment.

NEWHAVEN

Origin of name: established by James IV as alternative to the older port of Leith.
Government: (local) ward 11 (Trinity);
(national) Edinburgh North, Leith. Community council.

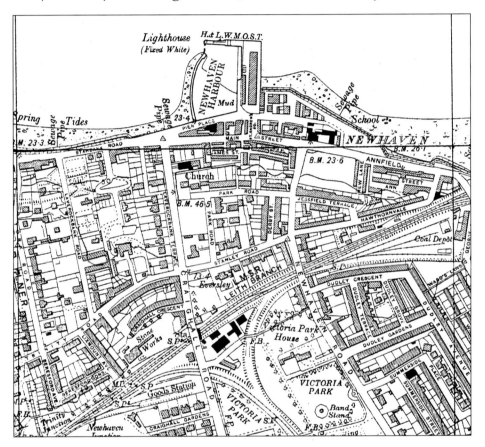

'Our port of grace' is a phrase well applied to Newhaven, a former fishing community which was originally created by James IV as a shipbuilding site to produce his mighty warship *Michael* at the beginning of the 16th century. James required a deep-water launch site for a ship which he intended as Europe's greatest. Five years in construction, the *Michael* was launched in October 1511, probably displacing around 1,000 tons, with a hull 150ft long and a crew of some 300. If James planned to use her to implement his expansionist plans, her career was to be short-lived. Within two years James had perished at Flodden, and his flagship was sold to the French for little more than half the cost of her construction.

Situated immediately west of Leith, Newhaven maintained its links with the sea as a fishing port, although the harbour was not constructed in its present form until the 1860s, with a fishmarket also being built on the eastern quay some 30 years later. The village rapidly became famous for its fishwives (although other Forth ports had them too). These were female vendors selling fish from door to door, carrying a creel on their backs, secured by a strap round the forehead. Their calls of 'Caller herrin' and 'Caller ou' [fresh herring, fresh oysters] were known throughout Edinburgh. They had another characteristic that was equally well-known; because of it the local railway station at Trinity had a separate booking-window for fishwives, and they were allotted their own compartments on the train!

Newhaven harbour is now given over to leisure sailing, and there is an interesting heritage museum and restaurant on the quayside. The village itself – something of a pantiled gem, well worth visiting – is now conserved and bypassed by the main Leith-Granton road.

The village has always been known for the quality of its inns and pubs. While Duddingston claims the oldest public house in the city, and Bruntsfield's Golf Tavern takes some beating for its antiquity, Newhaven boasts the Peacock Inn. Perhaps better known for its catering than its bar, the Peacock, once owned by the late Tommy Younger (an international Hibs goalkeeper made somewhat redundant by playing behind the Famous Five), remains one of Edinburgh's best watering-holes. Another Newhaven howff was Barney Battles Bar. Also owned by a former footballer, this time a 1920s international centre-forward for Hearts (and who represented the USA as well as Scotland), this hostelry was one for the connoisseurs of Scottish pubs, with an atmosphere closely reflecting the local environment, that of a genuine fishing village resisting gentrification. On his one and only visit, your author overheard one drinker say to another 'A telt the skipper, if ye ignore the spark near the fuel line we'll be the first trawler on the moon'.

Newhaven harbour dates from the first decade of the 16th century, when James IV chose this coastal site as perfect for the construction and launch of his planned flagship the Michael. *She, if that it is the correct pronoun, was launched in 1511, although the king's death at Flodden two years later inevitably shortened her working life. The present Newhaven harbour dates from the 1860s, although both the lighthouse and the fish market building (out of sight to the right) are later additions.*

Main Street Newhaven, as seen on a recent winter's day, is a pleasing change from the industrialised waterfronts of Leith to the east, and to a lesser extent, Granton to the west. A bypass now takes the heaviest traffic round the north of the village, giving some peace and quiet to the resident and inspiration to the visitor. Among visitors inspired by Newhaven were Charles Darwin and the artist/photographer David Octavius Hill.

Just to the west of the village, the Old Chain Pier Bar is another pub with a city-wide appeal. While it has lost much of its character, given it by previous owners with a notoriously eccentric taste in decoration, newer owners have made a much-needed alteration – putting windows in the back wall to create a glorious seascape for the tippler to enjoy.

One of the most distinguished visitors to Newhaven in centuries gone by was the young Charles Darwin, who found the littoral here to be a fertile source of biological specimens. How seaside research fitted in with his medical studies was never clear to Darwin's contemporaries, and his Edinburgh sojourn of 1826–7 tends to be dismissed by his biographers as having no influence on his development as one of science's most important workers – as if attendance at Britain's foremost scientific university of the time could have had no influence on his thinking! More probably, it was the later presence at Edinburgh University of his critic Professor Fleeming Jenkin, whose mechanistic arguments Darwin struggled to overcome in the sixth edition of his *Origin of Species*, which turned Darwin against his alma mater and ensured he never revisited it, or Newhaven and Joppa for that matter, where he drew his early inspiration.

Less than 20 years later, pioneering photographers David Octavius Hill and Robert Adamson produced 'sun pictures' of Newhaven's fishermen, and these are now regarded as among the finest early photographs ever created. Hill and Adamson were the outstanding photographers of their time – and all because of English and French inventors' inability to tell the difference between 'England' and 'Britain'. In patenting their photographic processes in London, both Louis Daguerre and Henry Fox Talbot were unaware that the Patent Office had no legal jurisdiction over Scotland at that time. Daguerre was exploiting his Daguerrotype (actually invented by Joseph Niepce), while England's Fox Talbot was the inventor of the more seminal Calotype, introducing the negative-positive process which dominated photography for nearly 150 years, and which was rapidly taken up by the artist Hill and his more technical colleague Adamson. They were able, quite legally, to use this process freely, although they had to commission their own cameras. Hill first used his to record the image of all the dissenting ministers who set up the new Free Kirk, at Tanfield in 1843 (see Canonmills).

If all this seems a little opportunistic, it should be recalled that the separate Patent Office in Scotland had no jurisdiction south of the border and that much-underrated physicist and inventor David Brewster saw his invention of the kaleidoscope pirated the length and breadth of England. Ironically, it was Brewster who introduced Hill and Adamson to each other in the first place. Brewster was not only the first to create movement in two dimensions (with his kaleidoscope) but saved countless numbers of lives worldwide by providing a theoretical means of improving lighthouse optics (actually implemented by the Frenchman Louis Fresnel). The Patent Office took on a UK mantle in 1852, but too late to benefit the unfortunate Brewster.

Close to the waterside is the 'Alien Rock', one of Scotland's most challenging indoor climbing centres, accommodated in a former church building. It overlooks the harbour, guarded by its Victorian lighthouse, where the author's father was 'taught' to swim by being thrown in, or so he later claimed.

NEWINGTON

*Origin of name: variant of Scots
word 'Newton',
meaning new farm.
Government: (local) wards 33
(Southside), 49 (Newington) and 50
(Prestonfield);
(national) Edinburgh South.
Covered only partially by Southside
community council.*

A district of contrasts. From the villas of Blacket and Blackford, to the tenements edging towards St Leonards, to the council housing of Prestonfield, this is more of a geographical expression than a community. Significantly, no community council has been founded in the largest, southern, part of the area.

While mainly residential, Newington has some light industries, although it is no longer the main centre for the city's printing and publishing, as it once was. The presses of Messrs Neil no longer operate in Mayfield Road, while Holyrood Road has lost the headquarters of Nelson's, and Duncan Street, that of Bartholomew's. Thomas Nelson's printing works was one of the most important in the UK, while Bartholomew's was probably the world's most famous independently-run mapmakers. This independence came to an end in 1985, when the owning family decided to sell to HarperCollins, and production was soon moved out of Edinburgh to the Glasgow area. The site – the former Geographical Institute – is now given over to housing, but Nelson's factory in Holyrood Park Road has been replaced by a new building, the headquarters of Scottish Widows. Designed by Sir Basil Spence, this interesting building, ringed by a moat of illuminated ponds, has been described by architect-historian Charles McKean as consisting of 'elephant proportioned glass hexagons'. He at least approved of the 'stunning landscaping by Sylvia Crowe'.

Newington district, looking from Blackford Hill towards Edinburgh's own volcano, the (thankfully) extinct Arthur's Seat. At 514ft, Blackford Hill is outranked by Arthur's Seat at 822ft, but both are familiar to city-dwellers as prominent viewpoints for looking over the city. On the skyline in the centre of the picture are Salisbury Crags, the inspiration for the description of Matto Grosso in Conan Doyle's The Lost World.

This south-side view may be unfamiliar as these buildings, fronted by Parker's haberdashery, were swept away in the late 1960s. This 1954 view was taken looking southwards from the end of Bristo Place. Nowadays, looking in the same direction would reveal a soulless plaza, with the Students' Centre to the left and the McEwan Hall to the right. Now the square echoes to the clatter of skateboards. (Edinburgh City Libraries)

As far back as 1932 the *Scotsman* newspaper complimented the insurance industry on its contribution to Edinburgh's distinctive skyline, and Spence's Widows building is undoubtedly one of the city's most attractive to be built in the 20th century. But the insurance (strictly speaking, mainly life assurance) companies have contributed others – principally the new Standard Life complex at Canonmills, built around Tanfield Hall, and in Lothian Road. Scottish Life built a less grandiose, but nevertheless interesting, office in Henderson Row, occupying the former site of the cable car depot, and displaying some of the winding equipment.

But it is Newington which interests us here, and at a site not far from where Nelson's printing works was located, and close to the location of the Commonwealth pool, once upon a time could be found Britain's most infamous school... St Trinian's! Strictly speaking, this was St Trinnean's, a progressive but comparatively nondescript private school, accommodated from 1925 to 1946 in St Leonard's House, built for Thomas Nelson himself. The school's notoriety stemmed from a wartime meeting between two of its female pupils and the cartoonist Ronald Searle, who drew some cartoons to illustrate their somewhat exaggerated accounts of the school's supposed awfulness. Following publication in the then popular magazine *Liliput*, Searle's work attracted the world of cinema, and a number of St Trinian's films were made. These starred Edinburgh's own Alastair Sim playing the headmistress in drag, with Sim's adopted son George Cole as the girls' personal bookie. Not surprisingly, the former headmistress of the real St Trinnean's, Miss Lee, found it necessary in 1962 to publish a true account of the school, pointedly called *The real St Trinnean's*, in order to clear the school's name!

For a suburb noted for its contribution to printing and publishing, it is highly fitting that Newington should have counted a certain Mr Roget among its residents in the 19th century. Roget is a name most associated with his *Thesaurus*, an encyclopaedic collection of synonyms designed to assist the writer seeking an appropriate word or phrase. Born into a London-based French family, Peter Mark Roget was moved by his family to Edinburgh, where he qualified in medicine at the tender age of 19. His widowed mother reportedly disliked the city, but conceded that living at the east end of the Burgh Muir was a pleasant enough location, and her frail son could walk to and from the university in a matter of minutes. He also spent a summer at South Queensferry, convalescing from TB. While he made an interesting contribution to medical science, speculating on the persistence of vision which is the basis of cinema, it is his *Thesaurus* which has immortalised his name. First published in 1852, this work, begun originally as a series of notes which Roget used to adorn his own writing, has never been out of print since, and is currently in its 19th edition.

The Royal Observatory Edinburgh (ROE) is topped by two domes, although 'drums' might be a better description of the two copper structures atop the 1896 complex of buildings on the east side of Blackford Hill. The farther away of these is 33ft in diameter, the nearer 22ft, but neither now houses an active telescope, so bad is the light pollution over Edinburgh. The nearer dome, or turret, houses a fascinating visitor centre, well worthy of a visit. ROE is now the technical centre for British astronomy.

From time to time, proposals emerge for the reopening of the city's Suburban Circle, and this photograph shows what commuters have been missing. This is an inner-circle train (that is, one leaving Waverley westwards and returning from the Portobello direction), headed by a V1 steam locomotive on a wintry March day in 1958. These machines were designed by Edinburgh's own Sir Nigel Gresley, more usually celebrated for his Flying Scotsman *and* Mallard *locomotives. (W.S. Sellar)*

To the north of Newington, and bordering on the city centre, is Edinburgh's new Festival Theatre. Situated opposite Surgeon's Hall, the glass atrium provides an interesting contrast to (and a good view of) the classical lines of the Surgeons' building. Theatre-goers may be slightly disappointed once inside the former Empire however, as the modernisation process is really restricted to the exterior. Nevertheless, the Festival Theatre has one of the largest stages in Europe, and is an important – and desperately needed – addition to the Edinburgh International Festival. Opened as the Empire Palace in 1892, this was a venue for variety entertainment, and even became Scotland's first cinema when a Kinetoscope show was included in a stage programme including performing dogs. In 1911 the theatre suffered a major fire, in which the internationally famous illusionist Lafayette perished, and the Empire embarked on a somewhat kenspeckle course through the 20th century, being sold for bingo in 1963.

A more theatrical use for such a large venue was long overdue, and city festival-goers breathed a collective sigh of relief when in 1991 the Empire was bought by a trust supported by the local authority and appropriate tourist and cultural agencies. Three years later the Festival Theatre opened, with seating reduced from the previous capacity of 2,016, but complete with its 900m^2 stage intact.

Not many British suburbs can claim a National Library in their midst, but Newington can. The Causewayside annexe of the National Library of Scotland can be found at the junction of Causewayside and Salisbury Place, built in 1987 to accommodate the science library, map division, and service areas. Unfortunately, the science library is now closed, a loss doubled by the fact that it also specialised in disseminating business and financial information. While much of a library's reference traffic can now be handled by online databases, there must still be a place where a scientific enquirer can undertake journal-based research; indeed there are some enquiries that simply cannot be punched into a one-line computer prompt box.

A leafy byway in the Newington area, looking towards Blackford Hill. Private gardens comprise an important part of the city's environment, one threatened by applications to tarmac over front gardens to gain vitally needed parking space for residents. This is because of the local authority's need to control parking in peripheral areas of the city, very much in demand by commuters who drive to Newington, Marchmont, and Morningside, park for the day, and take a bus into the city centre, but the policy also penalises local residents. A better transport system from the Lothians and Fife, particularly if rail-based, would reduce all-day suburban parking, save countless gardens, and lower CO_2 levels.

The science library was arguably not given enough opportunity to build up a client base among those whose scientific interests are not institutionally grounded – it opened only one evening per week, not at all on Saturday, and parking nearby was (and still is, for the map researcher) almost impossible. Happily the map division is still here, and does open on Saturdays. This book is all the better for the copies it has supplied, and for the professionalism of the staff. Nevertheless, the long-term planning of the National Library has always been flawed; a King's Buildings location – where one building site lay unoccupied for 15 years – might have been sought from the university, with consequent improvement in road access and parking. But what else can you expect from a nation which ignored the Royal Society of Edinburgh's offer of its entire science library to the Scottish public in 1969? (See this author's *Edinburgh Encyclopedia*, p.189)

To the west of Newington is Blackford, a south-side residential suburb which is frequently known as Blackford Hill, for the hill has played a major part in the development of the area, providing a base for the Royal Observatory.

Opened in 1896, the ROE is built within a walled compound whose principal features are two green copper domes (although drums would be a more accurate description) of 33ft and 22ft diameter respectively. These still dominate the skyline on Blackford Hill, from a height of 479ft (146m) in what is arguably one of Edinburgh's most interesting 'listed' buildings. The domes housed a 15-inch refractor and 24-inch reflector at the time of the opening, although neither dome now contains an active telescope. The observatory is now known as the technical

Architectural contrasts are very much in evidence in this picture showing, in the foreground, part of the Basil Spence-designed Scottish Widows building at Dalkeith Road, with the standard school architecture of Preston Street Primary in the background.

The Royal Commonwealth Pool was designed by Matthew Johnson-Marshall in time for the 1970 Commonwealth Games, and has served the city well ever since. With separate diving and children's areas, it caters for all levels of swimming proficiency, and has the now-obligatory leisure addition of a 'flume' system. Keeping up with the demands of ever-more complicated competitive swimming is less easy however, and the pool now figures in fewer competitive events than it once did.

centre for Britain's astronomical community, with technicians outnumbering scientists here. The UK's telescopes are mainly pointed at the skies over Hawaii and Australia as Blackford is heavily light-polluted. When you realise that city lighting can compromise astronomical observations from 120 miles away, it's understandable that Edinburgh can no longer be used for space surveying. The city council has hardly helped by refusing to adopt a dark skies policy in 1999; not what one might expect from a city of science and learning, making the city's acceptance of the European Space City Award for 2001 somewhat undeserved. Why shouldn't Edinburgh citizens be able to see the Milky Way from their own gardens?

At the south-east corner of the hill, in West Mains Road, can be found the British Geological Survey building. This is the nucleus of the nation's geological expertise, a science that has ceased to be merely academic as man probes deep into the mantle of his planet in search of minerals, and even places of safety to store his nuclear waste. Edinburgh has a proud history in furthering both the scientific and practical aspects of geology, the city being the birthplace of James Hutton.

Despite lacking a university background, Hutton was the Charles Darwin of geology, bravely postulating that a biblical timescale was hopelessly inadequate for measuring the age of the earth, and that geomorphological processes must

Clouds gather over Newington in this panoramic shot from the west end of the Queen's Drive in Holyrood Park. In the foreground can be seen the Pollock halls of residence, providing accommodation for Edinburgh University students, while the Royal Commonwealth Pool can be seen to the right. In the left middle area of the picture, the spire of Mayfield parish church points to Blackford Hill, with the Pentlands in the distance.

Edinburgh from the Queen's Park, with the Salisbury Crags on the right of the picture. This book is not about the city centre, but the view of the crags and the city is a visible reminder that Edinburgh has a beautiful location, not out of good fortune, but because the citizens wanted it that way. At one time the crags to the right were extensively quarried. In the 1820s city residents fought a court case to limit the amount of extraction which could take place there, arguing that the crags were a visual asset to the city. Thus was the modern civic movement born, with the Cockburn Association being formed some 50 years later, the first of its kind.

have begun millions, not a few thousand, years ago. His conclusions were contested by Gottleib Werner, whose Neptunian philosophy was championed, ironically in Edinburgh, by Leith-born William Jameson, Professor of Natural History at the university. Jameson turned out more Werneran students than Werner himself! Since Hutton had no students whom he could influence, it was left to others, principally John Playfair, to argue Hutton's case. History can forgive Jameson his misdirection – he donated a massive collection of natural history specimens to what is now the Royal Museum of Scotland.

Blackford Hill itself is a 514ft high example of a crag and tail formation, with, as observed in the introduction, the observatory in the 'Holyrood' position. The site is legally designated as a local nature reserve, although the city's policy of holding fireworks displays here hardly suggests a conservationist's conscience at the City Chambers. To the north of the hill is Blackford Quarry. Its main face is now infilled, but a smaller quarry remains, a haven for rock climbers (although a licence is required from the Countryside Rangers at nearby Hermitage House). The Agassiz Rock nearby is an example of ice-age striation, or not, depending on which geological expert you consult, but the valley, running westwards to Hermitage of Braid and Morningside, is well worth visiting anyway. The road approach to Blackford Hill from the eastern side is through the impressive Harrison arch commemorating Sir George Harrison, former Lord Provost and first MP for Edinburgh South.

Not many British suburbs can claim a National Library in their midst, but Newington can. This is the Causewayside annexe of the National Library of Scotland, built in 1987 to accommodate the science library, map division and service areas. Unfortunately, the science library is now closed, but the map researcher will still find this a treasure-house of information. The motorist should, however, be prepared for what might be a lengthy walk from the nearest parking-space.

NB: Information on Mark Roget taken from a highly informative article by John Dallas in his 'Physicians' Folios' column in *Scottish Book Collector*, Vol. 6, 2001.

PORTOBELLO

*Name: supposedly from the battle of Puerto Bello in Panama
in 1739, named by a survivor who settled near the mouth of
the Figgate Burn.*
*Government: (local) Burgh status until 1896, now Portobello
and Mountcastle wards;
(national) Edinburgh East and Musselburgh. Portobello
community council.*

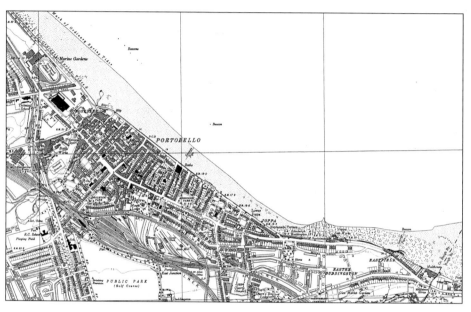

*Portobello High Street
hardly looks like this
now, being almost
permanently choked
with traffic despite the
opening of the Sir
Harry Lauder Road
bypass to the south.
This 1903 view is
looking westwards
from the top of Bath
Street, with the then
town hall with its
clock tower prominent.
'Porty' had ceased to
be an independent
burgh only seven years
previously, yet a new
town hall would later
be built (out of sight to
the left) and the
existing building would
become the combined
police station and
public library (the
latter now moved to a
custom-built structure
nearby). Quite what
the police officer is
saying to a member of
the public amid the
cable car tracks is
difficult to guess!
(Edinburgh City
Libraries)*

Once known as 'Edinburgh by the sea', Portobello (or Porty) is no longer one of
Scotland's favourite holiday resorts. A municipal burgh from 1833 to 1896, the
town always had an ambivalent attitude to the Firth of Forth which borders it to
the north and north-east. The existence of attractive sands, complemented for 40

years by a pier and for a longer period by a substantial funfair, never quite succeeded in ousting industry and commerce from the local consciousness. As a result, power station chimneys and pottery kilns were sited within yards of the beach, perfectly illustrating the divided nature of Portobello.

Originally known as Figgate Whins – an area notorious for being frequented by criminals ejected from the city of Edinburgh – Portobello developed mainly through its extractive industries, clay and sand. The former initiated a pottery industry, although this later used imported materials, only closing in the 1960s, while marine sand was used in bottle-making until around the same period. Salt was produced at Joppa Pans for many years, and a further connection with the sea was a small harbour, situated at the mouth of the Figgate (known inland as the Braid Burn), where boat-building once took place.

It was the sea which generated the next chapter in Portobello's history, with the wide sands providing enough room for cavalry manouevres attended by George IV in 1822, drawing attention to the town as a place where a pleasant summer's day could be spent. The arrival of the railway in the mid-1840s brought both excursionists and encouraged commuting, and this dual movement continued with the introduction of the trams late in the 19th century.

A fine indoor swimming pool was opened in 1893, and is still going strong, although the massive open-air pool, occupying the entire block immediately west of the mouth of the Figgate Burn, closed in 1978. Its closure was a final

Portobello open-air swimming pool opened in 1936 and closed in 1978. It provided a huge area of water – twice the area of the Royal Commonwealth Pool. Part of the Portobello complex was designated as a 15ft deep diving area underneath the 33ft tower. Hydraulic pistons provided waves on a regular basis, bathers being warned by klaxon before the pistons began their work.

admission that Porty would no longer attempt to compete in the holidaying, or even the fitness, markets. With an area twice that of the Commonwealth Pool, and a diving tower no less than 33ft high, it was the finest facility of its kind in Scotland. From its opening in May 1936 it was intended to have its water supply warmed and supplied from the power station next door – but this didn't seem to work in practice, as your hardy author cannot recall without a shiver! The opening was marked by the Lord Provost and its retinue having to flee from the poolside when the mechanical wave-maker, consisting of 24ft-long pistons – was demonstrated, proving more effective than anticipated. In later years a klaxon had to be sounded before this feature was used. With changing public tastes, or perhaps just a softening of the young of today, pools like this, and those at Port Seton and North Berwick, lost their popularity, but some consideration should surely have been given to roofing over the pool. Its site is now in the possession of five-a-side footballers.

Another attraction which failed to last was the pier, opened near the foot of Bath Street in 1879 and closed in 1917. A funfair was built on the site of the harbour until closure in 1970s and a huge leisure area at Seafield, known as the Marine Gardens, and boasting Britain's largest dance hall, also succumbed to changing social habits.

Portobello was never able to throw itself wholeheartedly into the idea of becoming a holiday resort. Admittedly, the climate is not helpful in this respect, but there was a conspicuous lack of investment in tourist facilities during the 20th century. Instead, a power station complete with 400ft chimney was allowed to dominate the area from the 1920s, with determined holidaymakers sitting almost in the shadow of the giant stack, until it became outmoded in the 1970s.

Previous page: Portobello's divided identity is summed up perfectly by this 1987 picture showing the redundant power station next to the closed open-air bathing pool. Although it was supposed to be 'the Brighton of the north', it's surely doubtful whether Brighton or any other self-respecting holiday resort would allow a coal-fired generating station to be built overlooking the beach! The 350ft-high stack succeeded in carrying smoke away from the immediate locality, but local people would be awakened in the early hours every morning by thunderous discharges of excess steam, which could be heard from two miles away. In the middle distance of this picture, the Figgate Burn (also known as the Braid) can be seen emerging from under the promenade and finding the sea.

Now the once-bustling High Street is almost overwhelmed by the warehousing and housing schemes to the south of the town hall which, curiously, was not finished until after Portobello lost its municipal status in 1896. (The previous town hall, a delight to architectural historians, is presently the police station, and there was an even earlier version housed in what it now the Baptist Church). Just to emphasise how times have changed, swimming was banned at Portobello Beach for a time in the late 1990s because of pollution.

While Craigentinny could hardly be regarded as part of Portobello, it would

Next page: This is the extant second town hall (the first now being used as the Baptist Church along the High Street), but is highly impressive, in its 'Franco-baronial' style dating from 1877.

Portobello promenade, shown in the Joppa area on an April evening in 1963. In those days every high tide came up to the promenade, so low was the sand level. Locals believed this was because of excessive extraction of sand for the Portobello bottle works, but whether true or not, dredged sand had to be brought to the area from the Fisherrow area in 1973 in an effort to restore Porty's credentials as a holiday resort. Inchkeith can be seen on the right skyline of this photograph, looking remarkably like a giant battleship.

Left: From the east, from the mouth of the Esk at Musselburgh, Edinburgh is represented by Arthur's Seat with Portobello on the shore below. The most prominent architectural feature in the middle of the picture is the spire of St Philip's Church at Joppa, but Nelson's Column and Scotland's Disgrace can just be glimpsed on the Calton Hill.

Right: Radar arrays tower over the bungalows of Milton Road East, from the 'upper deck' of the Jewel and Esk College. This establishment has taken over the mantle of the former Leith Nautical College. The 'Jewel' of the title is a reference to a fertile coal seam which once ran under this area and was accessed from a number of Midlothian mines.

Centre: One of the relief panels in marble on the side of this most neglected of suburban memorials just off the Portobello Road. Sculpted by Alfred Gatley, this commemorated the song of Moses and Miriam. One of the dancers nearest the camera appears to be playing the tambourine.

Bottom: The Craigentinny Marbles, a funerary monument to 19th-century landowner William Christie Miller, hidden on a side street off the Portobello Road.

be even more topographically challenging to place it in Duddingston, its traditional parish. This area of housing divides almost equally into privately built housing west of the railway, and council housing east of it. There is a substantial carriage depot here, stretching from the Figgate Park as far into town as Piershill. To historians the most interesting feature of Craigentinny is the funerary monument known as the Craigentinny Marbles, just off the Portobello Road.

Although almost unknown today, local landowner William Christie Miller guaranteed immortality for himself by being buried in a 20ft pit topped by this impressive monument, completed in 1856 with two panels illustrating biblical incidents.

RESTALRIG

Origin of name: disputed, possible variant of 'Lestalric', itself
of disputed origin.
Government: (local) ward 38 (Restalrig);
(national) Edinburgh East and Musselburgh. Not covered by
any one community council.

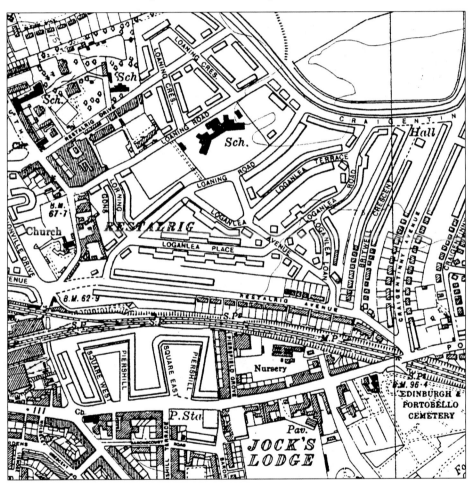

Another former village in its own right, Restalrig traces its roots back to the Middle Ages, when the local ruling family, the Logans, controlled much of Leith. Local antiquities include the intriguing Craigentinny House, Lochend House, and St Triduana's well, and there is still a recognisable village street.

St Triduana's is named for a saint who is reputed to have plucked out her own eyes and sent them to an unwelcome, and doubtless unnerved, admirer. Not surprisingly, the well's waters are believed to cure ocular problems, and its site was enclosed in the 15th century within a pitched vaulted structure 35 ft across. The building was restored in 1906, around which time the well ceased to be used.

The Logan home, Lochend House – a largely 18th-century replacement for the

Lochend pond at Restalrig, as seen on a summer evening in 1955. Once an attractive water feature, fed by an underground spring, the pond's location became a safety problem, with the construction nearby of so many high-density houses. Accidents led to the supposedly 'bottomless' pond being partially filled in, and it is now fenced for even greater safety. The idea of a local duckpond being fenced seems incredible at first sight, but the local authority can hardly be blamed for putting lives first. (Edinburgh City Libraries)

original 16th century building – overlooks Lochend Loch. Fed by subterranean springs, the loch provided a piped supply down the hill to Leith for a few years after 1753, before being superseded by the main supply from the Pentlands (although the Edinburgh authorities had a bad habit of cutting that off if rainfall in the hills had not met expectation). Lochend Loch subsequently earned a macabre reputation for being bottomless, probably because the bodies of

Another view of Lochend pond, with the doocot prominent. This still stands, having been part of the Logan family estate. The pond, having an underground source, was used to supply water to Leith, an arrangement which failed to work effectively, and was superseded by a pipeline from Edinburgh around 1771. Unfortunately, this supply would be cut off intentionally at times of drought, adding to the Edinburgh-Leith enmity that we keep hearing about! (Edinburgh City Libraries)

drowning victims were trapped by underwater ledges. The problem was acute enough for the loch to be partially filled in during the 1960s, and, as an additional safety precaution, the waterside is now fenced off. The appearance of this unsightly, if necessary, construction is partially softened by the growth of willow trees along the water's edge. A nearby dumpling-shaped building is a 16th-century doocot surviving from the original Logan estate.

Another ancient building of more than passing interest is Craigentinny Castle, whose very presence in an area of intensive council housing comes as a visual shock to the visitor. Constructed by the Nisbet family in the 16th century, with a stair tower prominent in one corner, it was partially rebuilt in early Victorian times, and is now used by local government for social work purposes. It is strictly speaking outside present-day Restalrig, but since the village of that name was the parochial superior for the whole of Leith, it is perhaps not stretching a point to include other areas of interest under this heading.

One such is the housing scheme off the Portobello Road immediately east of the brae running down from Jock's Lodge (a well-known pub) to Restalrig. The scheme was built in the 1930s on the site of Piershill Barracks, and the layout of the two squares preserves the memory of drilling squares. It was from here that dragoons rode forth in French Revolutionary and Napoleonic times to put down insurrections in outlying pit villages, sometimes bloodily.

Restalrig was a village situated south of Leith and was a larger community for many decades, governed by the local Logan family until the 17th century. It still has a recognisable village street today, although somewhat changed from this 1850 view looking south. It may have been taken on a special occasion, judging by some of the headwear on display. Restalrig holds a tiny place in aviation history, being the landing site of the first British balloon flight, which took off from nearby Abbeyhill in 1784. (Edinburgh City Libraries)

On the other side of the brae is Meadowbank House, the National Office of Sasines, a storehouse for conveyancing records made over the centuries. It was built on the site of St Margaret's locomotive depot, over which a pall of smoke hung for around 110 years, due to the steam locomotive's failure 'to consume its own smoke' as required by Act of Parliament. Nowadays, with steam locomotives merely a feature of the preserved railway branch-lines, it is surprising to recall that successive City Medical Officers pleaded for the closure of the depot, its smoky location barely 50 yards from the nearest tenement. With better railway management it should surely have been possible for overnight stabling to have taken place at an enlarged Seafield depot, with immediate servicing being done at the Haymarket site. Neither would have inflicted its smoke on a housing scheme nearby.

Surrounded by council housing to the north and east, and bungalow land to the south, Restalrig is an interesting relic of times past, and can claim a footnote in aeronautical history as the landing site of the first balloon flight on the British mainland (see Abbeyhill).

SAUGHTON

Origin of name: from 'Sauchie' or willowy farm.
Government: (local) wards 27 (Moat) and 28 (Stenhouse); (national) Edinburgh Central. Stenhouse and Hutchison/Chesser community councils.

Nowadays one of the most populous areas of Edinburgh, Saughton figures little in the city's histories. Originally part of St Cuthbert's parish, Saughton was detached from it by an act of the old Scottish Parliament and 'relocated' to Corstorphine parish in 1633. Now Saughton can be found roughly between Corstorphine and Craiglockhart on a north-south axis, and between Gorgie and the city boundary.

One of the area's greatest claims to posterity is that it was probably the site of one of Oliver Cromwell's rare defeats. On 27 August 1650 the Scottish army commanded by Sir Alexander Leslie confronted the Roundheads marching northwards from the Pentlands. Thanks to the boggy nature of the ground south of Corstorphine, Cromwell was unable to make progress in the face of artillery and small-arms fire.

Saughton is more than just the venue of Edinburgh's prison, and this picture reveals one of the area's most attractive corners. This is the main glasshouse in the Saughton Winter Garden, an attractive refuge from the cares of urban life, established in 1984. The bust of Mahatma Gandhi emphasises the cosmopolitan appeal of the garden.

The south-east entrance to Saughton Park is across this concrete footbridge at the junction of Balgreen and Gorgie Roads. Established in 1900, the park comprises 42 acres, including a fine collection of roses and the indoor Winter Garden, opened in 1984. The northern side of the park is given over to sport in this, one of the city's most important green spaces.

'Shaped gables and crenellations give a false jollity' runs the architectural description of Saughton Prison in the Penguin Buildings of Edinburgh guide, a description not many might agree with. Opened in 1925, the prison holds up to 600 inmates at one time, and includes a hospital and a training centre for rehabilitating prisoners. The last execution here took place in September 1951.

Opposite page: St Salvator's church in Stenhouse, between Saughton and Carricknowe, is a surprisingly recent addition to the cityscape. Construction began in 1939, based on a Fife ecclesiastical design at St Monan's, but it is not as large as intended when building ended in 1942.

He withdrew eastwards – but only temporarily. So over-confident were the Scots following this skirmish that they threw away a strategic advantage at the subsequent Battle of Dunbar, allowing Cromwell to trounce Leslie's army and return to Edinburgh in triumph.

Saughton expanded hugely in the period between World War One and Two, along with neighbouring Slateford and Stenhouse. It is perhaps best known to the outsider as the location of Edinburgh Prison, and although the area deserves to be better known for other things, the prison should be described. Its 36-acre site distinctive for being only partly walled, Saughton Prison opened in 1925, the

successor to the Calton Gaol where St Andrew's House now stands. The Penguin guide to Edinburgh's buildings describes its main block as 'harled with red sandstone dressings ... shaped gables and crenellations give a false jollity'. There would have been little jollity for those on death row anyway, Saughton being the site for capital punishment until 1951.

If nearby Corstorphine has the lion's share of westbound traffic passing through it, the Saughton area is not much better, being transected by the main road to Kilmarnock, with the Glasgow and Aberdeen railway lines separating at Saughton Junction, where Corstorphine's first station was sited. The line to Carstairs or Glasgow (Central) runs along the southern edge of the area, parallel with the Union Canal. Both of these modes of transport stride across the Water of Leith and Inglis Green Road just north of the Lanark Road.

Anyone travelling through the area may miss the Saughton Winter Garden next to the Water of Leith. Opened in 1984, and noted for its roses, the garden also has an impressive collection of glasshouse flora, and is well worth visiting. Next door, the sports enthusiast is well served, the traditional football pitches being supplemented by a new indoor sports centre.

SOUTH QUEENSFERRY

Origin of name: denotes ferry passage with royal imprimatur.
Government: (local) wards 3 (Dalmeny/Kirkliston) and 4
(South Queensferry);
(national) Edinburgh West. Queensferry community council.

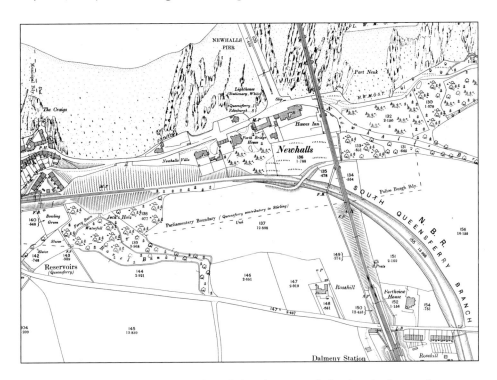

Separated from the rest of Edinburgh by the green belt, South Queensferry was added to the city's administrative area by the local government reorganisation of 1975. It was perhaps a surprising move, and one not entirely welcome in the town, up to that time a royal burgh. 'This loss of autonomy is still a matter of resentment; Queensferry still thinks of itself as part of West Lothian', advised the *Third Statistical Account* as recently as 1990. The former burgh is dominated by the two bridges spanning the Forth to the north, although local sources of employment were the distillery (although closed in 1985), the naval depot and minesweeping base at Port Edgar (the former reduced in size, the latter converted to leisure use), and a new electronics factory. This last-mentioned is a welcome addition to the local economy, and there is also employment to be had at the nearby tank farm and oil-loading utility at Hound Point (both strictly speaking in Dalmeny).

Central South Queensferry is now a conservation area, and architecturally very attractive. Much of the town's hinterland has become ringed with new housing, putting considerable pressure on schools and local facilities, as the town increasingly sees itself becoming an Edinburgh dormitory.

One of the West Lothian communities which passed into Edinburgh in the
1975 local government reorganisation, Dalmeny is a surprisingly large parish
almost enclosing South Queensferry to the north. Dalmeny village itself is centred
round a charming village green, with the Norman church nearby, its 1937 tower
perfectly blending with the rest of the 12th-century building. The Penguin guide
to the buildings of Scotland rates this as 'the best preserved Norman church in
the country'.

The village was boosted by the building of the Forth railway bridge in

An unusual view of the
Forth rail bridge, as
seen from the
pedestrian path on the
newer road structure.
It's easy to see what
Hamilton Ellis meant
when he wrote that the
Victorian bridge had
'an unconscious
beauty' as the camera
catches a coaster vessel
making its way up the
firth to Grangemouth,
and the supertankers
loading at Hound Point
behind. Imagine how
offensive this huge
structure would have
been had it not
exhibited an easy
grace!

1883–90, and the road bridge in 1959–64, and they provide the visitor to South Queensferry with a magnificent perspective. The older bridge is more interesting since it was very much 'cutting edge' for its time, and was begun not long after the collapse of the original Tay Bridge in 1879. Indeed, the designer of the latter, Sir Thomas Bouch, was already constructing a rail bridge over the Forth, a nightmare monstrosity comprising a tubular viaduct slung from chains suspended from 500ft-high towers! Not unnaturally, the collapse of the Tay structure caused construction on the Forth to stop, although the records show that the chains still had to be paid for.

Within a few years, pressure from English railway companies forged a new consortium to bridge the Forth, although at a height greater than the constructors would have liked, the tracks being no less than 150ft above high tide, allowing all but the largest naval vessels to pass beneath. With new designers – John Fowler and Benjamin Baker – appointed, and a cantilever design chosen, a seven-year building programme began, in which 57 men died. Despite the death toll, unacceptable by modern standards, it was a triumph for Victorian engineering, and has produced

Low cloud needs to
come down to little
more than 400ft or so
to obscure the tops of
the towers of the Forth
road bridge. Completed
in 1964, the bridge is
something of a victim
of its own success, its
predicted vehicle-
carrying turnover long
ago exceeded, and the
need for greater
carriageway capacity
great.

The Hawes Inn at South Queensferry in 1905. Situated beside the ferry ramp, the inn was an integral part of the Scottish transport scene, and this changed little even after the opening of the rail bridge, seen above, in 1890. As motor transport came into its own in the mid-20th century, this would often be a scene for admittance to one of the drive-on ferries, rather than make the long journey round via Kincardine. The opening of the Forth road bridge in 1964 changed all that. (Edinburgh City Libraries)

a structure which has been described by one architectural critic as 'unconsciously beautiful'. One can imagine how unpleasant it would have been if such a huge addition to the landscape had not been beautiful at all, but fortunately the aesthete need not feel offended. It is quite a construction, considering that the consortium's first board meeting had to be abandoned for being inquorate.

One little-known fact about this famous structure is its history of illegality. When the constructing company, the Forth Bridge Railway Co., was absorbed into a larger company in 1923, it was discovered that Scottish company laws were not being adhered to, individual directors having to personally own shares in the FBR even if they were representing client railways using the bridge. This would have been perfectly easy to comply with, but appears not have been, even after the discrepancy came to light. The fact that all board meetings came to be held in London's Marylebone for the next 25 years ensured that Scottish legislation continued to be ignored! The bridge was nationalised in 1948, but is now in the tender care of Railtrack Scotland.

The newer road bridge is less distinctive, although properly administered, and is impressive enough in its own right. If it was being built nowadays, probably six traffic lanes would be provided, but lack of capacity is probably the only criticism that can be levelled at it.

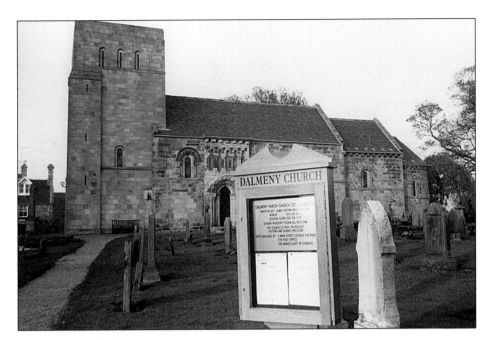

St Cuthbert's church at Dalmeny dates from Norman times, but its west tower was sensitively added as recently as 1937. Now part of the Edinburgh local authority area, this place of worship, along with Kirkliston's, rivals Duddingston in its antiquity and fine record of continuous service to its local faithful.

While the constructors have moved on, so has the military, with its extensive depot at Dalmeny. The tank farm is carefully landscaped, making less of a mark on the landscape than might otherwise be feared. Otherwise, Dalmeny, like its neighbouring community of South Queensferry, is fast becoming an Edinburgh dormitory.

STOCKBRIDGE

Origin of name: from Anglian 'Stocc Brycg', meaning a wooden bridge.
Government: (local) wards 8 (Comely Bank), 16 (Dean) and (17) Stockbridge;
(national) divided by Edinburgh Central, West, North and Leith. Community council.

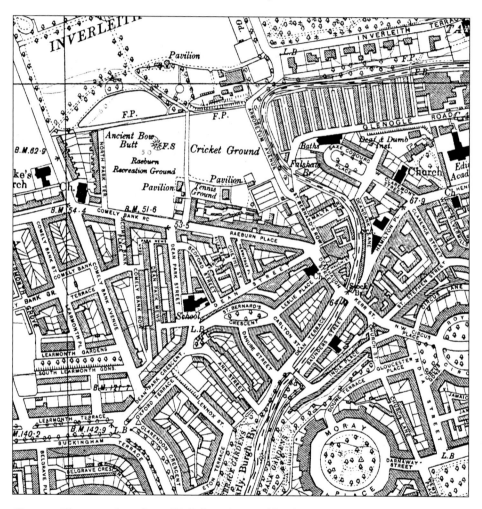

Once a village on the edge of Edinburgh, Stockbridge now enjoys a reputation for being one of the most cosmopolitan and intriguing areas of the city. Straddling the Water of Leith west of Canonmills, and not a mile from the city's West End, 'Stockaree' offers the visitor a wide range of exotic shops including The Lighting Museum in St Stephen's Street, as well as an array of pubs, restaurants and shops catering for alternative lifestyles. No longer centred around its market, although its southern archway never fails to intrigue the visitor, the area has its own theatre – the highly-rated Theatre Workshop. Inverleith park and pond can be found just

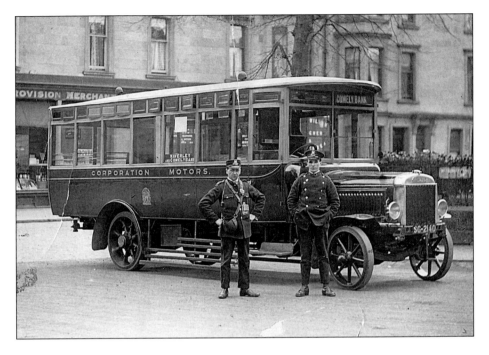

The Stockbridge and Comely Bank areas always posed problems for the unfortunate horses used on the early bus services, as well as all other traffic. Not unnaturally this led to cable car services being pioneered out of Stockbridge, but these were coming to an end around the city when this picture was taken of a Leyland bus and its crew in East Fettes Avenue in 1921. One wonders what kind of journey the passengers would experience on the way up to Waverley in a bus which appears from this photograph to have no rubber tyres! (Edinburgh City Libraries)

beyond the sports grounds off Gilmore Place – cricket on the right of Portgower Place, rugby to the left, and the Royal Botanic Garden is immediately to the north.

The RBG spreads over 75 acres in its third location since being founded as a medicinal garden for the university in 1670 (see Canongate). The present

A nanny walks her charges in the area of Inverleith Park, at around the end of the 19th century. The gate piers in the background were designed with rusticated detail by Sydney Mitchell; they would be difficult to see from this angle nowadays because of the presence of parked cars and ice-cream vans. (Edinburgh City Libraries)

location is Inverleith, with the house of that name as its centrepiece on a hill commanding a magnificent view southwards to the city skyline. The garden is now a national – as opposed to exclusively university – responsibility, and employs over 200 staff. The collection here comprises more than 300 plant families and 2,800 genera, as well as the UK's oldest botanical library and a herbarium containing more than two million specimens.

But the 'Botanics' is more than just a recital of scientific statistics; it is a haven of peace and quiet in the busy capital, and all the better for being free to everyone. The glasshouses are particularly worthy of note, one of them being the tallest of its kind in Britain, and all kinds of climatic conditions – from rain forest to arid desert – are simulated. But the extensive rock garden and lily pond are two of the most popular parts of the garden, an attraction which no visitor to the city should miss.

Included in Stockbridge is Comely Bank, an almost wholly tenement area. As the Marchmont of north Edinburgh, Comely Bank surely does not deserve a reputation for snobbishness and genteel behaviour often also attributed to Morningside. The area is really a western adjunct of Stockbridge, with Inverleith Park, Fettes, and the Western General Hospital to the north. The naming of its

primary school, for Flora Stevenson, pioneering Edinburgh educationalist, is a pleasant touch.

The Dean Village, just westwards along the river, is dealt with under Haymarket. On the way to it, the walker cannot fail to be impressed by St

Stockbridge from the south, with a cable car heading downhill towards the Water of Leith bridge, with its bank building which is such a feature of the townscape. St Stephen's Street, is out of sight to the right. (Edinburgh City Libraries)

Stockbridge market closed in 1906. The archway remains, incorporated into a housing area, and with a right of way through to Hamilton Place. Opened in 1826, Stockbridge market appears to have been a challenge to the town council, which controlled trading in the city at the time, and it has a parallel in Broughton market. (Edinburgh City Libraries)

It's stretching things a little to place Fettes College in Stockbridge, but this 1960s view is worthy of inclusion. Founded in 1870, Fettes currently enjoys having Prime Minister Tony Blair as one of its 'old boys', and was selected by author Ian Fleming as just the sort of place that James Bond would have attended. Ironically, when Sean Connery visited here regularly it was to deliver milk. (Edinburgh City Libraries)

The Royal Botanic Garden is one of the finest jewels in Edinburgh's crown. Instituted in the 17th century to serve the university's demand for medicinal herbs, its story is told under three different areas in this book, under Canongate, where it was first established at St Ann's Yards, the Waverley Station area, where it 'called' near the present-day platform 11, and Broughton, where it was situated on a five-acre site before moving to Inverleith near Stockbridge in 1822.

Bernard's Well, situated by the riverside and visible from India Place bridge. The well is enclosed in a striking mock-Roman temple commissioned by Lord Gardenstone in 1788 and built by Alexander Nasmyth, the landscape painter. Although famed for its good all-round healthy qualities, the well no longer produces sulphurous waters. The authors of the standard book on Scotland's wells, Ruth and Frank Morris, find it necessary (in *Scottish Healing Wells*, 1982) to warn well-seekers that not all of the nation's water sources are as dignified as St Bernard's!

TOLLCROSS

Government: (local) wards 31 (Fountainbridge)
and 32 (Tollcross);
(national) Edinburgh Central. Active community council.

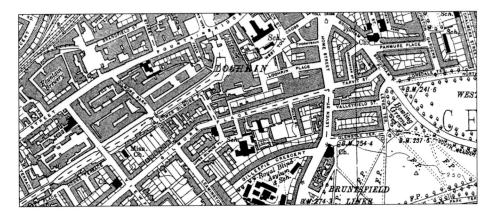

Tollcross is almost near enough to the city centre to be regarded as part of it – yet the local population, the most cosmopolitan in Edinburgh, rightly regards Tollcross as a community in its own right. Tollcross, as its name implies, is a crossroads on a major road, in this case the A702 to Dumfries from here, but it also sends out tentacles across the Meadows to Newington, through Fountainbridge to Dalry, and up to Lauriston. Once a major shopping centre, Tollcross has lost many of the smaller shops which gave it such a variety of attractions, especially in Earl Grey Street.

Edinburgh's most cosmopolitan community, Tollcross has changed considerably in the years since World War Two. The loss of such industries as the rubber factories, slaughterhouses, co-operative warehousing, and a reduction in brewing, is reflected in the opening-up of the centre of Tollcross, with the eastern side of

Leamington lift bridge spans the Union Canal off Gilmore Place, guarding the truncated final basin immediately south and west of West Fountainbridge. The bridge originally carried that very thoroughfare across the waterway, but was moved in the mid-20th century to allow Fountainbridge to be expanded. The steel structure contained an operator's cabin within the casing, as well as a pedestrian bridge to allow people across even when the bridge had been lifted to the top of its (not terribly high) lifting range.

A more atmospheric shot of the Leamington bridge when actually in place at Fountainbridge. This is a southward view, the canal turning right after passing under the road, and heading parallel to Gilmore Place, then westwards to Grangemouth. Pictured here in 1920, the canal was cut back to the other side of Fountainbridge some two years later, exactly a century after its opening. (Edinburgh City Libraries)

Earl Grey Street demolished in the early 1970s to facilitate traffic flow. (The eastern pavement now boasts an isolated extension of the West End's new office complex).

The convergence of a number of traffic thoroughfares on Tollcross certainly justifies the local history of the area being published under the title *By Three Great Roads*. Here the A702 heading south to the M6 or Dumfries is met by Brougham Place, named for locally born slavery abolitionist Lord Brougham, this latter thoroughfare having crossed the Meadows from Newington. From the present Royal Infirmary, Lauriston Place comes down into the crossroads, and there are two one-way streets connecting north-westwards to West Fountainbridge. There is, however, another transport utility.

The historic Union Canal constitutes an almost forgotten means of travelling westwards out of Edinburgh. While the original basin has long gone, buried under Lothian House and the Regal/ABC cinema, the foreshortened waterway (presently ending close to the former Palais in West Fountainbridge) is frequently the focus of property speculators wishing to make a canal basin the centrepiece of new office developments. And who can blame them – up to now Edinburgh has made little of its canal heritage, compared to such cities as London or Birmingham. This was the spot where Charles Darwin stepped 'ashore' when he arrived to attend Edinburgh University in 1825, so a potential canal heritage remains to be developed.

Tollcross plays an integral part in the city's ability to fight the scourge of all cities – fire. At Lauriston Place the Lothian and Borders Fire Brigade has its headquarters. Once an active fire station, the building here, hiding the Art College from the street, is now the administrative headquarters of the force, as well as housing the Museum of Fire. Down in Tollcross itself is a newer (1986) fire station graced by 'a swirling geometric stone façade to the street' as described by author-architect Charles McKean, and occupying the site immediately next door to the former tram depot.

Looking west from the Leamington lift bridge on a winter's day in early 2001, along the frozen Union Canal. The waterway's last commercial function was not transport, but water supply, serving the rubber industry on a 22-acre Castle Mills site to the right of the photograph. 4,400 employees worked here half a century ago producing all types of rubber goods, from golf balls to tyres. Nowadays, the building on the right is part of the brewing complex still giving employment to local people. Needless to say, canal water is not part of the process, and recreational use is likely to be the future for this once-vital transport artery.

Although not strictly part of Tollcross, the Regal/ABC cinema is too interesting not to include in a survey of the area. Built in the late 1930s on one of Edinburgh's famous 'holes in the ground' – the site of the former Port Hopetoun canal basin – the Regal was one of the city's most popular first-run cinemas, even before becoming the first in Edinburgh to 'triple' its auditorium, in 1969. Presently closed for extensive rebuilding, the Regal is still remembered for a frantic stage appearance by the Beatles in 1964, and a rather quieter visit from the illustrious Hollywood actor Jack Lemmon, whom local filmgoers failed to recognise as he strolled out of the cinema into Lothian Road after attending a premiere.

Edinburgh was one of the first British cities to fight fire systematically and professionally – as one might expect of a community which has given the UK some of its greatest life assurance companies. Its pioneering 19th-century firemaster, James Braidwood, was so highly thought of that he was lured away to London after only nine years in the post. During his tenure in Edinburgh (1824–33) he introduced a high level of training, requiring staff to abseil down the North Bridge, and established a network of hand-operated mobile appliances which could be transported to a blaze in the minimum time possible. He went on to serve London for a further 28 years, dying when actively joining his men in fighting a major conflagration.

Tollcross still has its Fountain Brewery. Occupying 22 acres, this opened as recently as 1973, representing a rationalisation of existing facilities. Motorists on the Lanark Road may not know that they are travelling underneath a beer pipe taking the amber nectar to a kegging plant on the Haymarket side of Dundee Street! The historic McEwan's Clock is situated here, a colourful addition to an otherwise featureless street.

The variety of of shops and places of entertainments in Tollcross is not as great as it was. Former attractions included such retailers as Goldberg's, now demolished, but which brought Sunday shopping to the capital, and the Palladium, the Coliseum (later the Palais ballroom), and such cinemas as the King's (Cameo), the Beverley (Blue Halls), and Tollcross, to say nothing of the King's Theatre.

The last named, although not the city's oldest or largest theatre, is one which is held in the greatest affection by Edinburgh citizens. It reaches out to thousands every winter with its highly popular pantomime, while playing its part as a more

cultural centre during the Edinburgh International Festival. Completed in 1906, with the contractor in financial difficulties, it was snapped up by the Howard and Wyndham Company (who already owned the Lyceum), and has prospered ever since. Curiously, both the Edinburgh architectural guides quoted in this book describe the King's as 'rather Glaswegian', something about which the reader will have to make up their own mind. Originally accommodating 1,800, this was reduced by 200 with the closure of the 'Gods' in 1951, and now stands at 1,300 seats, but the King's can equal the Royal Lyceum for a sense of cosy intimacy.

While on the subject of show business, Fountainbridge can claim to be the birthplace of Scotland's most famous film actor, none other than Tom Connery, rather better known to the world as Sean Connery, and even better-known as the first, and undoubtedly the best, James Bond.

Connery came from humble origins, and unlike many successful members of the film industry, never forgot them, delighting in reminiscing about delivering milk around the city (to, among other places, Tony Blair's alma mater, Fettes College). He even worked as a lifeguard at Portobello's open-air pool, and was no doubt popular with lady bathers, having embarked on a body-building course. This soon opened the door of the acting profession to him, where he found that, in combination with his physical appearance, he could time a line to perfection. Star of seven Bond films, his fans' only regret may be that he failed to become involved in their creative side, perhaps commissioning his own Bond scripts – something he belatedly did only once, with *Never Say Never Again* in 1983. Edinburgh folk have nothing but pride in Sean's achievements, however – when he was awarded the Freedom of the City in 1991, the Usher Hall could have been filled nine times over.

With Tollcross so intensively built up as it is, it's curious to think that that the *First Statistical Account* lists the west end of Fountainbridge as the westernmost portion of the city of Edinburgh in 1792, with countryside between it and the

village of Dalry. In fact the local government ward of Tollcross stretches eastwards through the Grassmarket as far as the George IV Bridge, but this account has concentrated more on the western area, since that relates more to a sense of 'suburb', even if most local people would regard Tollcross as being about as central as you can be!

WESTER HAILES

Government: (local) ward 41 (Murrayburn);
(national) Edinburgh West. Community council designated but
not formed.

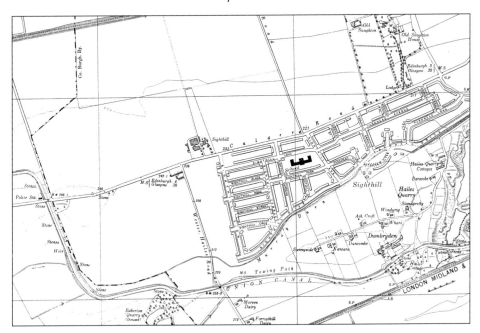

Described by architect-author Charles McKean as a 'dense 4,800-house township for expatriate Leithers plonked on Pentland foothills in tall white vaguely Scots fortresses', Wester Hailes was open country until 1966. The foothills were part of Colinton parish from 1636, stretching north from that village as far as the parochial boundary, the Murray Burn, a tributary of the Water of Leith. Now this is one of the principal council house areas in the city, its 11,000 population giving it almost the status of a satellite town. The scheme had few of a town's facilities when first built, unfortunately, 'the youth and teenagers being forgotten completely' [by the planners] commented Diana Sinclair, author of *Wester Hailes, A Sense of History*.

Gradually, living conditions improved, an excellent education centre being added which doubles as a sports and community facility. The housing in the area is now undergoing a regeneration, particularly of its 25 tower blocks, six of which are being reclad and the rest demolished. A railway station and (excellent) public library have opened in recent years, and more attention is being given to the need to generate community awareness. Yet, the almost piecemeal manner of trying to create a community at Wester Hailes, without commensurate retail and social facilities from the beginning, shows that the lessons of Pilton and Muirhouse had simply not been learned.

Wester Hailes centre is a commercial mall boxed by a public library on one

Until recently, this view eastwards from Murrayburn Road, in the heart of Wester Hailes, would have failed to reveal the Union Canal, which was culverted at this point. Now it is opened up for recreational traffic and for the traditional British habit of throwing bread to swans and ducks.

Wester Hailes centre, comprising shops, a cinema, community facilities and a public library, is perhaps not to everyone's architectural taste, but boring it certainly is not. With the railway station situated immediately to the south, and buses visiting the north side of the centre, transport to and from the rest of Edinburgh is not as much of a problem as it might have been, considering the comparative remoteness of this council estate.

side, multi-screen cinema on the western side opposite, and canal and railway to north and south respectively. The canal has been literally reopened here, converted from its former culverted state; the station is on the line between Waverley and Glasgow (Central) via Shotts, or Carlisle. With a little imagination it surely should be possible to run trains between here and Newcraighall via the Suburban line south of the city.

The visitor to Wester Hailes can hardly fail to notice that the placename 'Murrayburn' occurs on buildings and street signs there as much as the name chosen for the development. Perhaps the city authorities, in selecting 'Wester Hailes' for the new complex, were hoping to provide Edinburgh with symmetrical parameters. For, on the eastern side of the city, just north of Newcraighall, and immediately east of Joppa, is New Hailes. It is near enough semantically to 'Wester Hailes' to neatly 'book end' the city!

APPENDIX

WARD (No. & Title)		COVERED BY CHAPTER
1	Balerno	Balerno
2	Baberton	Currie
3	Dalmeny/Kirkliston	South Queensferry/Kirkliston
4	Queensferry	South Queensferry
5	Cramond	Cramond
6	Davidson's Mains	Davidson's Mains
7	Muirhouse/Drylaw	Granton
8	Craigleith	Blackhall
9	Pilton	Granton
10	Granton	Granton
11	Trinity	Newhaven
12	Newhaven	Newhaven
13	East Craigs	Corstorphine
14	NE Corstorphine	Corstorphine
15	Murrayfield	Murrayfield/Haymarket
16	Dean	Stockbridge
17	Stockbridge	Stockbridge
18	New Town	(Various)
19	Broughton	Broughton
20	Calton	Canongate
21	Harbour	Leith
22	Lorne	Leith
23	Gyle	Corstorphine
24	SE Corstorphine	Corstorphine
25	Parkhead	Wester Hailes
26	Craiglockhart	Craiglockhart
27	Stenhouse	Murrayfield
28	Moat	Craiglockhart
29	Shandon	Merchiston
30	Dalry	Dalry/Haymarket
31	Fountainbridge	Tollcross
32	Tollcross	Tollcross
33	Southside	Canongate
34	Holyrood	Canongate
35	Meadowbank	Restalrig
36	Mountcastle	Portobello
37	Leith Links	Leith
38	Restalrig	Restalrig
39	Portobello	Portobello
40	Milton	Portobello

41	Murrayburn	Wester Hailes
42	Sighthill	Saughton
43	Colinton	Colinton
44	Firhill	Fairmilehead
45	Merchiston	Merchiston
46	N Morningside/Grange	Morningside/Marchmont
47	Marchmont	Marchmont
48	Sciennes	Marchmont
49	Newington	Newington
50	Prestonfield	Newington
51	S Morningside	Morningside
52	Fairmilehead	Fairmilehead
53	Alnwickhill	Liberton
54	Kaimes	Liberton
55	Moredun	Gilmerton
56	Gilmerton	Gilmerton
57	Craigmillar	Craigmillar
58	Duddingston	Duddingston

BIBLIOGRAPHY

Baird, G. *Edinburgh's theatres, cinemas and circuses* (Available in Edinburgh City Libraries).

Baird, W. *Annals of Duddingston and Portobello,* 1898.

Baldwin, J. *Exploring Scotland's Heritage: Edinburgh, Lothians and the Borders* Stationery Office, 1997.

Brotchie, A. *The Twilight years of the Edinburgh tram* Adam Gordon, 2001.

Cant, M. *Edinburgh: Gorgie and Dalry,* 1995.

—— *Marchmont, Sciennes and the Grange,* 2001.

—— *Villages of Edinburgh: An illustrated guide* (2 vols).

Coghill, H. *Discovering the Water of Leith* John Donald, 1988.

Gifford, J. et al. *Edinburgh (Buildings of Scotland)* Penguin, 1984.

Harris, S. *The place names of Edinburgh; their origins and history* Gordon Wright, 1996.

Jeffrey, A. *This present emergency* Mainstream, 1992.

McBain, J. *Pictures Past* Moorfoot, 1984.

McKean, C. *Edinburgh: an illustrated architectural guide* RIAS, 1992.

McKenzie, R. *Hearts: the official history* Breedon Publishing, 2001.

McWilliam, C. *Lothian (Buildings of Scotland)* Penguin, 1978.

Mullay, S. *Edinburgh Encyclopedia* Mainstream, 1996.

Smith, G.D. *The Scottish Beer Bible* Mercat Press, 2001.

Thomas, B. *The Last Picture Shows, Edinburgh* Moorfoot, 1983.